D1500632

Closing the Chasm:

Letters from a Bipolar Physician to His Son

Benjamin Diven, MD

iUniverse, Inc.
New York   Bloomington

Closing the Chasm
Letters from a bipolar doctor to his son

iUniverse books may be ordered through booksellers or by contacting:

iUniverse
1663 Liberty Drive
Bloomington, IN 47403
www.iuniverse.com
1-800-Authors (1-800-288-4677)

Because of the dynamic nature of the Internet, any Web addresses or links contained in this book may have changed since publication and may no longer be valid. The views expressed in this work are solely those of the author and do not necessarily reflect the views of the publisher, and the publisher hereby disclaims any responsibility for them.

ISBN: 978-0-595-48109-5 (soft)
ISBN: 978-0-595-60207-0 (ebook)

Printed in the United States of America

iUniverse rev. date: 1/20/2009

Dedication

For Elinor, Matt, Ryan, and Callie

Epigraph

I felt a cleavage in my mind
As if my brain had split;
I tried to match it, seam by seam,
But could not make them fit.

The thought behind I strove to join
Unto the thought before,
But sequence ravelled out of reach
Like balls upon a floor.

Emily Dickinson

Contents

Preface

This is a story about me. It is a work of nonfiction. The story concerns my thirty-seven years of battling a major mental illness. At times I leave it to the reader to sort out fact from fiction, although I've done my very best to avoid fiction; the facts are troublesome enough.

As with all mental illnesses (mine is manic-depressive illness or bipolar disorder), the crazy times are difficult to recall accurately or concisely. Facts can take a beating in this kind of work. I have had to lean heavily on an imperfect ability to recall events. Digging through old photographs has been valuable. Life has been strange and colorful. I'm looking back now from a long period of stability and clarity.

Acknowledgments

Front cover photograph by Elinor Diven, used with permission Author photograph by Jack Diven, Jack Diven Photography, used with permission Epigraph © Bartlesby.com, Inc., used with permission Cover design by Bob Diven, Bob Diven Art, used with permission

Introduction

Imagine a mental illness that includes euphoric highs and boundless energy and confidence—an illness that allows you to live on little or no sleep while you concoct and carry out grandiose and elaborate schemes. This pattern of behavior is called mania. If that was all that this disorder involved, no one would seek treatment, and few could criticize him or her for not doing so. People would love living with a person with this disorder. But there is a rub to this euphoria. It usually turns into depression sooner or later, and the highs become awful lows. Even the euphoric high times often lead to overspending and sexual misadventures. Severe anxiety is common. Crazy plans become enormous failures, and relationships suffer. The disorder becomes destructive in all of its phases. This is bipolar disorder or manic-depressive disease. I've suffered from it for all of my adult life.

Bipolar disorder is a unique major mental illness. Its characteristic mood swings have made it the oldest mental disorder described in medical history. The pattern was readily recognized and recorded. It often starts in the late teenage years and may fully develop in the twenties. It is a lifelong illness that has no cure. The origin of the illness is obscure, though it has a tendency to be inherited. Children of bipolar patients have a moderate risk for developing a major mood disorder. Bipolar disorder comes in a few different forms, but the symptoms are remarkably consistent among them. I have an unusual form but generally conventional symptoms.

Still, bipolar disorder affects each of its victims in a unique way.

Some are devastated by the disorder and struggle to live a near-normal life. The suicide rate is frighteningly high. Others become high-performing individuals when the high or manic phase allows for unusual productivity and creativity. For me the disorder has brought periods of pain and chaos as well as periods of energy and accomplishment. Although the disease can be isolating and alienating, I've always had the right person available to me at every critical juncture in the course of my illness to help see me through that crisis. Many have weathered this illness; some have done a better job than others.

Depression is a common disease and familiar to many. Treatments are numerous and are usually affordable and often effective. Mania is only seen in bipolar disorder and is much less common. The combination of these two features creates bipolar illness. As with depression the treatments are many, but they are often expensive, and many are ineffective. It is a difficult illness to manage. It is a difficult disease to live with.

Why You?

Dear Matt,

Out of our three kids you probably have the most experience with my mental illness and peculiar behaviors. Having a mental illness is like being in an earthquake. Where do you run to escape when the very ground is rumbling under your feet? I've only been in one earthquake. I was in San Francisco, and it caused a terrible feeling of helplessness. I was one of the few out-of-town attendees at a meeting, and I was out of my seat in a second. I was scared out of my wits. No one else even moved. The speaker's only comment was, "Next slide, please." I appeared to be alone in my sudden fear and attempt to escape the inescapable. That is what it is like when your mind rebels and you experience a major mental illness. There is nowhere to go to escape, and no one else is in your mind to witness it.

I've had bipolar disorder all of my adult life. This means you grew up with a mentally ill father. For most of your life we didn't know I was mentally ill. For years you lived with my peculiar moods with no explanation to help you understand or cope. Your younger siblings, Ryan and Callie, shared many of your experiences. But by the time they were old enough to understand, I had a diagnosis and was in therapy.

I wanted to write this book in the form of letters to you. As the eldest you are the best recipient. You are at least partially correct when you say that you were our parenting guinea pig. I don't think I've been

1

the best parent. During your entire childhood you were faced with inexperienced parents and a mentally ill father. We've had our rough times. Despite that situation I think you have, as your brother and sister have, loved and accepted me.

My father built a lot of myths about himself that I never fully understood. I know I've tried to make a legend of myself as well at times. I would have welcomed my dad's honest autobiography. I hope this book helps tear down some of my myths and gives you enlightenment both about me and about yourself. I hope the same for your siblings and your mother.

It won't be that long until you guys are parents. Parenthood is when you really start to examine your own upbringing. I'm trying to be ahead of the game. I hope this will give you a chance to be a better parent than I was and save you some therapy bills down the road.

Your loving father,
Dad

I took this photograph of you, Matt, while you were a graduate
student in Fort Collins in 2006.

Dead Dad

Dear Matt,

Speaking of my father, he died in 2006 of lung and heart failure and probably a huge stroke. Our last conversation was on a Tuesday morning. He couldn't talk very well through his oxygen mask and breathing machine, but I understood that the nurse had forgotten to put his dentures back in. I couldn't find them. I think he actually had them in. He went into a coma later that morning and died on Friday with all of us sitting around watching his last breaths.

I don't know how I felt about his death. I had long ago given up on having a heart-to-heart conversation with my dad. I had held out some hope that some day, perhaps in a hospital, he and I could clear up some things. We never did. But I wasn't particularly sad when he died. I may have been relieved.

My dad died with lots of secrets. I could almost see the secrets taking his breath away. He had so many hidden hurts they may have finally worn him out. He was ninety-two, so they certainly took their time getting him. Still, I think he spent a lot of energy keeping his secrets from everyone. I was just one of his five kids and one of many people who didn't know him particularly well.

For years I felt that he had a lot to apologize for, but he never got around to doing it. I would have liked one apology in particular. The day before Easter 1965, when I was eleven, my father took all of us kids to a florist to buy my mother flowers. My father picked out a pretty single lily in a small pot. It was nearly two feet tall. While he paid for the flower I carried it out to the car. The pot was much too small to hold such a tall flower, and it simply fell over out of the pot and landed on the ground. I was standing over the crushed lily holding the empty pot when my father came out of the store. I was shaking in my shoes with fear. My brothers were silent.

"What happened?" he asked angrily.

"It fell out of the pot," I said. "I didn't do anything."

That was enough for my dad. He lit up like a Roman candle. He proceeded to curse me to within an inch of the asphalt. I hid in my room for three days, and we didn't talk for weeks. The lily incident, however trivial it appears now, proved pivotal in my relationship with my dead dad. We spoke little after that about any subject, and I never brought up the incident. Would he have lived longer if he had had a chance to recall that day and apologize? That idea seems ridiculous, but I know we would have had a better parting.

My dad wasn't an evil man. I loved him. But I'm not sure I liked him. He probably did the best he could with what he had; he just didn't have a lot. His upbringing with an alcoholic and abusive father did little to prepare him for children or intimacy. Nevertheless, his impact on my life can't be understated. From big things to little things, I reflect my dad. Shortly after his death I was nailing up molding in the kitchen. I tapped on the points of the nails before driving them, just like my dad taught me. I get the itch to go out for coffee every afternoon about three o'clock, just like he did. He was sulky if he didn't get sex when he wanted, just like me. Guess where I picked up that trait? My disorder and my personality brought some of the same problems to your upbringing that he brought to mine. I hope I did a better job as a father than my father did, but how can I measure that?

My father didn't die happily or prepared. Death came on him suddenly and for all of us unexpectedly. I hope before my time comes we have had those important conversations that will fill in the many cracks in life I've left for you. I hope these letters help in that regard.

Your loving father,
Dad

You and my dad in 1982.

Growing Up

Dear Matt,

I thought my letters would make more sense to you if I included some description of my growing up. It isn't a favorite subject of mine, but issues from childhood inevitably come up in a work like this. I think of bipolar disorder as deranged brain chemicals causing psychological symptoms. According to some that makes my upbringing a moot point, as I am bound to have problems no matter what. However, I've learned to be more open to the idea that my formative years play a role in my disorder.

I was born and grew up in an Illinois farming town of two thousand people. It wasn't a bad place for a kid. I was the middle one of five boys. Every time I read something about middle children it seems I fit the profile. Five boys overwhelmed my parents, and I recall realizing fairly early in life that I had to take care of myself. My dad taught high school, and my mother hired housekeepers and babysitters to help her raise us and keep the small house we lived in livable. I think we stressed her to her limits.

My dad always had some project in the works. He was something of an inventor and creator of many works in wood. He always won the town Christmas decoration contest with moving displays using electric motors and lights. I don't know how much he was involved with us. I mostly remember running with my crowd of friends and our various caretakers. I think often we lived more off of my wealthy grandfather than my dad's more modest salary. My mother had been raised in wealth. Relatively speaking, so was I. We had the appearance of affluence, though I'm not sure we ever really had the substance. I spend when I'm manic, and it isn't hard to see where I learned that.

Let me give you an example of our "affluent" lifestyle by describing Christmas. I hated Christmas. The holiday was emotionally loaded at our house. Christmas season started with catalogs from the big department stores, like Sears. We would pick out everything a kid could possibly want with the expectation that Santa would deliver the goods. And the goods were delivered. We started with generous gifts at my grandparents' on Christmas Eve and took the impressive booty home, only to repeat the process of opening dozens of gifts the next morning. The recriminations had started by the next month. My parents couldn't possibly afford this holiday, and they borrowed money every year to finance the largesse. This made them angry toward one another, and it was obvious that Christmas was to blame. I enjoyed the toys, but I hated the follow-up after their arrival. I eventually quit enjoying any of it and dreaded the holiday altogether. I still do.

We moved to Las Cruces, New Mexico, when I was ten, and family life steadily deteriorated. My mother sunk into a chronic depression that didn't lift for years. My dad became even more distant and busy with his many projects and work. He spent many of his summers away at academic programs. I discovered girls very early, and my pattern of treating them like sex objects was evident from the start. Sex figures prominently in my mania.

My brothers and I just muddled through adolescence the best we could. There wasn't much parental involvement or guidance. I think my parents muddled through in the same way. I left home as soon as I could.

Once I'd left home I only saw my family periodically for the next couple years. My mother visited yearly. I did see my younger brothers, Jack and Bob, occasionally, as well as my older brother, Chuck, who was in the air force. I only saw my oldest brother, Bill, when I went home to visit. I feel like I grew closer to them during this time.

I don't think I was abused, though I feel like my needs were often neglected. My parents had their share of issues, and child rearing was not a skill they ever mastered. I can look back and see what may be the roots of some of my bipolar behaviors, particularly my spending, my borrowing, my hypersexuality, and my depressive symptoms. I don't think my upbringing is at the heart of my disorder, but learning about its influence on me over the years has helped fill in a lot of the cracks that I've stumbled onto while trying to understand my disease.

Your loving father,
Dad

Me as a child in the 1950s

Sixteen Going On Seventeen

Dear Matt,

I had my first episode of bipolar disorder when I was sixteen and a junior at Las Cruces High School. It was a wall-banging depression. At the time, 1970, I was a thoroughly disinterested honors student. I had grown my hair long and protested the Vietnam War. I smoked dope whenever I could get it, which was often, and enjoyed rock-and-roll music and girls. I didn't give a damn about much else. Your young future mother was a high school student two hundred miles away. She was beautiful and smart and wouldn't have given me a second look. It was only four years until we would meet.

It is common for bipolar disorder to start out with an episode of depression. My depression came on quickly and with no warning symptoms. It was as if I just woke up depressed one morning. I felt as if I had a hangover from all of life. I wasn't suffering from just the blues; I was suffering in a dark, deep place that had close walls. In very little time I ached with despair and feelings of hopelessness and helplessness. I soon felt suicidal.

All of this occurred for no discernible reason. My girlfriend, Janet, hadn't left me; I wasn't being thrown out of school or into jail. My parents certainly hadn't suddenly discovered their third son and begun to make life any worse than it already was. They were more tangled up in their problems than usual. I was just desperately depressed. Every little thing became a burden. I dragged myself wraithlike into school every day and got further and further behind academically.

You would think that such a sudden change would have been pretty apparent. It may have gone unnoticed largely because the moods of any teenager fluctuate like the phases of the moon. My depression could have looked like one more "down" in an already moody adolescent. My best friends thought feeling depressed was a normal state of mind most of the time, and I would have agreed with them if I had never experienced the real thing. My girlfriend didn't really notice much change.

"All you're interested in is sex. What's new about that?" she asked.

It was true that I remained interested in sex and drugs. But I was lost and alone in one black sea of grief-like hell. As a teenager I felt like I had a limited capacity to manage this type of mood swing. I had no clue as to the cause of my symptoms, and truthfully I wasn't even sure that anything was wrong with me. The world just sucked. As much trouble as mania has given me in my life, only anxiety has been as incapacitating as this depression. Fortunately this particular episode had a happy ending.

Your loving father,
Dad

What Happened In Chemistry Class

Dear Matt,

I took honors chemistry during my year of depression. The class caused me grief even before the depression started. I had no business being in honors chemistry in the first place, and my weak grasp on a passing grade was made all the more tenuous by my depression. Even my lab partner had to work hard to keep my lab reports from flunking us both out of the class.

"Our data doesn't fit the answers to the experiment," he would often say.

"Did we even do that experiment?" I would ask. "I don't remember doing it."

To make matters worse, the teacher, Frank Johnson, had assigned his legendary semester project: the poisoned jug. The project consisted of clarifying and purifying a gallon of polluted water. Not only did we have to return it to drinkable status, we had to be able to describe the pollutants and how we removed each one. The ugly jar sat on my lab desk for weeks. I was no more capable of completing the assignment than I was of taking a flying leap to the moon.

Mr. Johnson was an imposing figure despite his short stature and slight build. He was generally stern and walked around with a lab coat buttoned all the way up. He sported a bow tie. Mr. Johnson's manner wasn't gruff, but he was loud and forthright, and he seemed to know everything that went on in the classroom. He scared the begeebies out of me.

One Friday afternoon Mr. Johnson loudly announced at the end of class that he wanted me to come in the following morning for a special "session" with him. The class gasped. This unprecedented action could only mean that I was about to be moved to regular chemistry or face flunking the semester. My depression may have been unnoticed, but my poor grades were surprisingly public. I was frightened, but by then, what did I care? What could happen that could make me feel worse? Still, I dreaded every minute until I arrived the following morning.

It rained that Saturday morning. My 1941 Jeep didn't have a top, so I was pretty damp when I trudged into the classroom with my jar of charcoal-colored water, assuming that was the reason for our meeting. I wore my customary ratty military field jacket. Mr. Johnson sat at his little desk and didn't seem to notice my arrival. I took my seat. Eventually Mr. Johnson sighed, put down his pencil, and assumed an upright posture. He came over to my seat and sat in the desk next to mine. I don't recall exactly what he said, but it came out something like this: "Are you okay?"

"Yeah," I would have said. "Sure."

He didn't let me off the hook easily. "I mean are you really okay? You look and act so sad; I have trouble imagining how you're getting through school. Your grades are as depressed as you seem to be." He looked at me closely from not a foot away. "What's going on?"

"I don't know," I said. "I'm just feeling bad." I don't actually know if I even admitted that much.

He asked about home and my girlfriend and my drug use and the girl who sat in front of me (a beautiful, buxom girl who was the daily topic of conversation between my lab partner and me). I answered repeatedly that nothing was wrong. I just didn't feel good. He finally seemed satisfied.

"I wanted to make sure there wasn't something wrong that I could help you with," I think he said. "You know, trouble at home, that kind of thing."

"No," I said. I think I may have been more honest with Mr. Johnson during this exchange than I now remember.

"I want you to know that I want to help to you. Whatever I can do, I want you to let me know. Your partner will help you with your lousy lab reports, and I'll do what I can to help you through class. But I want to know about anything I can help you with outside of class as well."

I might have said thanks. I was so dumbfounded by Mr. Johnson's concern I probably just mumbled something. He put his small hand on my shoulder and looked at the charcoal-colored water in my jar. "You didn't try rinsing it with charcoal, did you?" he asked.

"Yes," I said.

"You didn't wash the charcoal first. Try that next time."

I never did purify the water or get a second date with the pretty girl who sat in front of me. Mr. Johnson stayed true to his word and often called me up to his desk so he could "look at my grades." He would quietly ask how I was doing and tell me to stare at the grade book.

This went on for months until I changed back to my old self. As rapidly as the depression had settled on me it evaporated in the spring of 1971. Depression is like that. It was as if the lights everywhere had been replaced with gigawatt bulbs and even the sun shone brighter. I regained my ability to focus on something beside my dark moods. Any thoughts of suicide vanished. I was relieved beyond joy. I soon had a new girlfriend. The previous one, Janet, had grown tired of my incessant sexual advances.

"I thought depression killed your sex drive," she said.

"Not mine."

Mr. Johnson told me he could see a change in my behavior in class and in the quality of my work. We quit having our small counseling sessions by the grade book. In my entire life I have met few persons who measure up to my opinion of Frank Johnson. I ran into him years after he had retired, and I had the chance to tell him this story and thank him. What do you think he said to that?

"It was just my job."

Your loving father,
Dad

This was taken of me during the homecoming bonfire in the middle of my depression in 1970. I recall the burden of depression that evening rather clearly.

TERROS

Dear Matt,

I left home after high school in 1972. I finished as I started: an honors student. I was accepted to Arizona State University the same way: with honors. I never have known what to make of all this honors stuff. If I was in the top tier of students at my high school I can only imagine how bored and disinterested the rest of the student body must have been.

I found a dump of an apartment in Phoenix the week before I graduated and moved right after walking across the platform. Alicia, my girlfriend when I graduated, was no longer my girlfriend when I moved. She had planned on moving with me but stood me up on graduation night, and we settled into a lopsided on-and-off relationship that dragged on for years. I was the one who remained interested. In fact, she was the only woman I ever asked to marry me besides your mother.

I spent graduation night in my Jeep parked on a hill above the new hospital, smoking dope. Sex and dope were largely all I was interested in those days, and I felt bad about spending the night alone. Still, that all-American misery of high school was over, and it was hard not to feel some relief.

Girl or no girl, I packed into my little car and went to Arizona that week. I was moving primarily to work at a street drug program named TERROS. The person who named the place thought *terros* was the Latin word for earth. I think the word is *terra*. TERROS ran an emergency drug treatment program complete with ambulances and offered training as an emergency medical technician. I was very interested in driving around in an ambulance taking care of overdoses and bad LSD trips. The program also operated a free clinic a couple evenings a week and a twenty-four hour telephone number for callers with drug or personal problems. I liked the idea of that too.

During my lousy high school years I had helped set up two crisis centers to offer the public access to urgent psychological counseling. These were popular in the late 1960s and were often called hotlines. In the couple years that we operated these programs, few people called or came by. Most were in a minor crisis due to circumstances or drugs. Because high school students staffed the centers it was probably a good thing that there were few callers. We could have had sex on any given shift with little worry about interruption. Serious suicidal or emotional crisis cases may have been better served by calling a wrong number.

I started at TERROS that summer as a volunteer and eventually became a paid staff member. I was good at what I did. No one ever asked if I was an honors student. College kept me busy on the side but was never the primary focus of my life. Life consisted of sex, drugs, and TERROS. I felt like I could have all I wanted of all three.

I was particularly interested in sex. Mania in bipolar disorder is supposed to cause hypersexuality, but I don't think mania was driving me at the time. I was just a constantly aroused teenager. There was a rule at TERROS that staff would abstain from drug use during their tenure. This was part of our "No Heat" policy. That rule was uniformly ignored. You just didn't go to work stoned. The police didn't interfere with our business, which was fundamental to the successful operations of TERROS.

The years I lived in Phoenix were tumultuous. I experienced the pain of growing up and did a lot of stupid things. I don't think much of it can be blamed on anything but age and inexperience. I grew my hair nearly to my belt loops. I was very proud of my hair. I still have my ponytail in a pickle jar. You found that pickle jar.

"What is this?" you asked.

"That's my hair. I used to have a ponytail."

"You had this much hair?" you asked. That was all you said.

TERROS proved to be a great place for me to grow and learn about myself. I also learned what a selfish little jerk I could be. My relationships with girls were fraught with my self-satisfaction and little kindness or true love. Hedonism was the name of my game.

TERROS was also my first real exposure to persons as patients. I liked it. I loved the excitement of emergency medical care and driving screaming ambulances through the streets. I had a lot of friends. I saw a lot of girls. I got tangled up in a commune for a while that was chockablock full of encounter groups and encouraged a *more* hedonistic lifestyle. I wasn't very good at the former, but I excelled at the latter. The longer I stayed at TERROS the more I enjoyed it and the lifestyle it afforded. Several doctors volunteered in our free clinic. They would come in their new cars and bring their girlfriends, never their wives.

"You guys have really got a good thing going here," they would say. "Chicks, drugs, freedom."

"Whoa, man," we would say. "You're the one with the Ferrari and the girls. You've got the money."

"You pay a stiff price for all of this stuff. You have a practice and employees and insurance companies and patients to put up with."

We silently agreed with them. We thought they were a sad lot who didn't seem to have any pleasure in what they did. Before long I decided that whatever became of me I would never become a physician.

Your loving father,
Dad

My TERROS identification card

Tripping Down
The Midnight Highway

Dear Matt,

During my long-haired hippie years at TERROS I enjoyed just about anything I could smoke or swallow. I particularly enjoyed amphetamines or "speed," as we called them. I can hear the voice of my first psychiatrist saying that bipolar patients will do anything to have more mania, and taking speed is as close to taking a mania pill as you can get. I thought I took it because I enjoyed it. But I think that the drug was tapping into my deeper mind and tickling at the mania that was later to blossom on its own. I may have proved that theory one night with the help of my mother.

My mother was depressed much of her life. When I was in high school she just lay on the couch day after day. She and my father rarely spoke. Is it any wonder my high school depression went unnoticed at home? I was a lightweight compared to her. During high school I avoided home for the most part. Avoiding her was easy; she was usually asleep. I've treated patients like her over the years, and I think now that the doctors she saw recognized her depression but didn't take her too seriously. They shoved all kinds of pills at her, but I don't know that she was ever really treated for depression. One of the pills they gave her was an amphetamine, a potent stimulant or "upper." She called the medicine her "diet pill." She didn't need to be on a diet.

I visited Las Cruces occasionally. It wasn't that long of a drive, and I had friends and Alicia to visit. I was still trying to win her back. I stayed away from home most of the time I was in town. During my second year away, sometime in 1973, I returned for a short visit. When I was ready to drive back to Phoenix I swallowed a couple of my mother's amphetamines. It was midnight.

Driving at night while taking speed was like wearing night vision goggles. I was wide-awake and feeling energetic. The world looked good. As I sped west I came up on a shiny new tanker truck. It was one of those made of polished aluminum, and I could easily see my reflection in the rear of the tank. Given my sharpened sight and speeding mind, I was quick to notice something odd about my reflection. I saw my car stretching out into the darkness as far as the horizon behind me. My face looked twisted and distorted in the glare of my headlights. This didn't disturb me at that time. I started to pass the truck.

As I came around the side of the truck it began to distort. It started to stretch until I couldn't see either end of it. The reflective truck tank gleamed as far as the dark horizons. It shone like a crystal finish. I could see every tiny detail of my car in the polished metal. My reflection was vivid and colorful. By this time I was beginning to feel really strange. I sped up. The truck seemed to stretch as fast as I could pass it. I was making slow progress and getting increasingly anxious about having a really bad experience with amphetamines and this truck. I went faster. I recklessly ignored the possibility of traffic coming up ahead of me. The truck just kept stretching. I could see my long slender car glistening in the polished sides of the tanker.

I became scared. I was frightened of this truck, to be sure, but I was even more certain I was having a bad trip on speed, and I wasn't supposed to have *any* trip on speed. Speed wasn't supposed to cause hallucinations. It never had before. It was doing it now.

I raced that truck for miles. Finally, little by little, the cab of the truck came into view. It was bright red, and it was distorted just like the rest of the tanker. ARKANSAS TRUCKING. I reached the door of the cab. The inside was invisible to me, but I pictured a ghostly figure at the wheel laughing demonically as he raced me down the interstate. Suddenly the truck was behind me.

I was sweating all over. My heart was racing, and my mind was filled with thoughts banging around the walls of my skull like marbles. I continued through the dark at over a hundred miles per hour, putting the truck lights rapidly behind me. Adding to the strange night atmosphere, there was no other traffic.

I was going to run out of gas.

I pulled into a beaten-down gas station I knew of right off the freeway. A friendly night attendant named Ray often operated the old station. Ray was probably the last clubfooted man in America. He was always cheerful at any hour. Ray came lumbering out immediately. I was a frantic wreck. I was certain that at any time that tanker truck was going to appear, crashing through the railing of the freeway and into the gas station in a massive fireball.

Ray was probably his usual cheerful self, but his efforts at conversation only struck me as ways of delaying my departure. He was somehow part of the conspiracy to incinerate me in a fiery truck wreck. He took a long time to reset the pump. He finally did it at my impatient insistence, and I quickly started pumping gas, trying unsuccessfully to calculate the minimum I needed to get home. My mind was racing too fast to manage the simple math. I just stopped pumping and gave Ray five dollars.

"Keep the change, Ray. I gotta go," I said.

I jumped back into the car with my eye on the freeway overhead. Ray slapped the trunk of the car and shouted, "Come again."

The speed trip lasted through the night and much of the next day while I hid in my old garage apartment in Phoenix. I finally settled down the next evening and slept like the dead. I'd missed a day of classes and almost missed a work shift the following morning.

Nothing about the crazy night made sense at that time. It makes sense now. I was already prone to mania, and the amphetamines had merely triggered a psychotic manic episode. I had no way of knowing that at that time, but the thought had crossed my mind that I might be unusually sensitive to amphetamines. I didn't take that thought very far. I just quit taking amphetamines.

Your loving father,
Dad

Dissociation And Sex

Dear Matt,

I lived in Arizona for two years. Hanging out with a hippie crowd made for a lot of adventures. They were generally a pretty bright and talented bunch of persons. Drugs or the war had burned out some of them, but they functioned well in our funny little place called TERROS. The word had nothing to do with Earth, but it did seem to have its own gravity that drew us all into its orbit.

The same winter of the terrifying truck incident, a girl came to my door wanting to spend the weekend with me. She came with a small shoulder bag. She had adopted the name of Robin, taken from the *Winnie the Pooh* stories. At the time I was out of school and working on a very poor novel. I knew almost from the start that it was going to be an unpalatable book. I had this drive to write, though, and I took the semester off just to work at TERROS and compose the novel. There was a hint of mania in how I attacked writing, going at it for days at a time with few breaks. I drank and smoked dope when I wasn't writing. All I had was a new manual portable typewriter, but I could whip out the pages one after the other. I'd frequently trash chapters at a time but have them replaced within hours. Writing was exhilarating, and I was enjoying the intensity of it. I only took long breaks to go to work.

The girl at my door was very attractive, with long straight hair and a petite figure. She had a lovely face that encouraged kissing. We were not strangers. We had been intimate in high school but had never quite gotten around to "doing it." She had previously expressed her desire to have sex with me but had never gone so far as to set up an almost infallible plan to accomplish it. She had come to Phoenix with a friend who had dropped her off and left. She, the girl at my door, had nowhere to go or stay. There was a reason we had never gotten down to having sex. I didn't trust this girl, and her motives with me always seemed to have a more permanent flavor than I liked.

"Ah, hi," I said.

"Hi."

"Gee, long time no see. What are you doing in town?" I asked. I looked over her shoulder and didn't see a car. "How did you get here?"

"I came with Ellen. She has some friends she wanted to see, so I just tagged along."

"Oh."

"Do you mind if I stay with you for the weekend? Ellen isn't coming back for me until Sunday. I don't know where she's staying," she said.

"Oh." My mind raced through the implications of what she was asking. I felt a brief pang of anxiety. It passed.

"Sure, come on in," I said.

What this girl's arrival had to do with what happened subsequently is not clear. There may be no connection. My first psychiatrist thought they were inseparable. It was a weekend of drinking, smoking dope, and sex. But as soon as she was gone on Sunday I was immediately back to the typewriter. The following evening while I thought I was writing, I suddenly and unexpectedly "woke up" to discover that I was driving down the freeway near Chandler, Arizona. The experience was identical to being rudely awakened from sleep. I hadn't been sleeping. I had been doing something, and at that moment the something was driving seventy-five miles an hour down Interstate 10. I was thirty miles from home, nearing a place I had visited only once before. It was about 2:00 AM, no time to visit Chandler under any pretense. The last moments I could distinctly remember were around 11:00 PM. I don't recall anything out of the ordinary happening. I just blanked out for three hours.

At first pass this may not seem like that big a deal to you, but think about it. Imagine for a minute a hole in your memory three hours long.

25

You can do a lot of things in three hours. I had no clues as to what I'd been doing or where I'd been. I had not done any drug or drank any alcohol that day. What had I been doing, and why couldn't I remember it? I was afraid to look in the trunk and discover something like a body and a gun. It was that weird. I stopped the car and stood in the chilly night air. I was dumbfounded. Was this a flashback? I had never heard of a blank memory being caused by a flashback. It was a new, unique, and entirely troubling experience.

Years later I learned that this was called dissociation. Dissociation is psychobabble for being unaware of what is happening for minutes to hours. The psychiatrist who told me that was sure it had to do with my intense ambivalence about the weekend with the girl. I didn't think my ambivalence had been all that great—certainly not enough to lose my mind temporarily. This phenomenon was to recur from time to time until I was adequately medicated for my bipolar disorder. Coming on the heels of the amphetamine trip, the whole episode was especially disturbing.

I got back in the car and drove home and went to bed. My bedroom still had the girl's aroma. It was a comfortable smell and not one that made me want to block out my memory.

Your loving father,
Dad

This was taken of me over Christmas the same winter as the bad amphetamine trip.

Trying Professional Help

Dear Matt,

Not long after I started school at Arizona State, my depressive symptoms recurred. The episode did not seem as dramatic as in high school. I was feeling sad, mostly, and indifferent to my life. I was having trouble developing new relationships even at TERROS. Being away from home was new. But I was frightened that I was heading back into a terrible depression like I had been through before. I think now that Alicia was at least one factor. She hinted at moving to Phoenix to be with me, but we were still emotionally distant and no longer physically intimate. I was not over her yet. Still, it felt like the depressive symptoms had a deeper cause—like they may have been the reason for and not the result of my struggles. I wonder now if it wasn't a mild recurrence of bipolar depression.

What surprises me is that I considered calling the university's counseling center. I had never sought professional care for an emotional problem in my life, and I had already been through one horrendous episode of depression. In high school I had been fodder for the analyst's couch. Still, I was reluctant to call a counselor but felt at the same time that I needed one. I had done "counseling" with patients in my days with the hotlines in the '60s, and I was starting to do some at TERROS. Perhaps that was the impetus. Whatever the reason, I decided I needed to talk to a professional.

I've found that people who work in counseling centers and

psychiatrists' offices must be screened to be certain that they always sound like you are the most important thing that has happened in their day. They act as though your concern is a matter of great concern to them.

Eventually I was facing the large open waiting room of Allen Hall at Arizona State's student counseling center. The double doors I had come through and the large blackboard at the end of the room gave me the distinct impression I had walked in on a class. I was ready to bolt at any moment. The chairs were arranged in rows on a large rug. They faced an old wooden desk where a young woman sat, much like a teacher in front of her students. I had to be in the wrong place. It had taken every bit of my meager courage to make the appointment and walk up the stairs and through the door. Calling for an appointment had reminded me of trying to make a date with some new girl who I was afraid would laugh out loud at the invitation. I can't count how many times I picked up the phone and then dropped it again. When I finally made contact, the voice on the other end was soft and sympathetic sounding.

"University counseling center. How can I help you?" the lovely voice asked.

"I would like to see someone," I said after an uncomfortably long pause.

"You would like to make an appointment? I could do that for you now."

"Yes," I said. "I'd like to do that." And I did.

Now I was standing at the receptionist's desk. The woman at the desk looked up at me. Her expression said, "Come in, make yourself comfortable." I couldn't resist her look. She looked as lovely as she had sounded on the phone.

"Good afternoon, Mr. Diven," she said quietly. "You are here for your three o'clock appointment." I didn't know if that was a question or a statement.

"Yes," I croaked.

"Please take a seat. We'll be with you very soon," she said softly.

Without looking at anyone else in the room, I found the one chair equidistant from everyone else who was waiting. I tried to look very sane. Eventually a smiling, sort of round man came to the room and called my name. He introduced himself to me: "John Guzman." My mind went completely blank.

Your loving father,
Dad

John Guzman

Dear Matt,

Visiting John Guzman was the beginning of an adulthood later dominated by professional counseling and psychiatry. Except for the first years of marriage and medical school and the gap following the misadventure with my next therapist, I've been in someone's appointment book for over twenty-two years.

I wish I could remember more of my time with John Guzman. He was a wonderfully open and warm man who took me seriously from my first visit. His office was small and quiet and lined with dark bookcases. We sat at the end of the room in chairs by a table with a lamp. He had clocks everywhere so he could time our visit to the minute. Psychiatrists do this also and are good at hiding clocks behind your head so you can't even see them looking at them. My present psychiatrist, Dr. B., is different. His brain works in thirty-minute cycles. He doesn't have to look at a clock. When he scribbles his finishing notes and signs the chart it has been exactly thirty minutes. I time him.

John Guzman and I saw each other for nearly two years. My depression symptoms persisted throughout that time. We didn't talk them away.

"How is the depression?" he would ask.

"It's doing well. I'm not," I would often answer. I thought it was a funny response.

Most of the time we talked about the issues in my life: drugs, sex, relationships, and my work. I don't think school was ever an issue. I didn't pay it enough attention. We rarely got into deeper matters like my childhood or my family. I didn't pay them much attention either.

It wasn't that I didn't hear from my family. My dad had a routine of writing to all his distant sons every Sunday afternoon. His letters were collections of sentence fragments attached to one another by ellipses.

During the time I saw John Guzman my life was definitely better because of his counsel. I developed many friendships during that time, and some were pretty close. My relationships with girls were plagued by my preoccupation with sex and my lousy efforts at intimacy of any other kind. He tried to help me there too, with little success. Still, I came to depend on him considerably. It was hard not to develop a lot of affection for this short round guy.

John tried to put me in group therapy. He thought I would do well in that setting. I was awful. My desire to act and sound saner than everyone else in the room led me to be coldly critical of other students' statements. I thought I was in a room full of whiners. It was okay that I visited John Guzman weekly and whined, but it wasn't okay if anyone else did. There was a very attractive girl in the group who was a worse actor than I was. I tried to take her out. She would have nothing to do with me.

No great problems were solved during my time with John Guzman, but I'm not sure that was what I needed at the time. The big problems were yet to come. He helped me at the right time to make the most of the life I was living and the mistakes I was making. John Guzman just did his job. He didn't step out of his expected role like Frank Johnson did. Still, he was the right person at the right time for me. It would happen repeatedly that the right person for me would come along just when I needed them. Thank you, John Guzman, wherever you are.

Your loving father,
Dad

Taken of me during a staff meeting at TERROS in 1973

Finally Getting The Signs

Dear Matt,

Not long after I turned twenty in the spring of 1974 I decided to become a doctor. This has proven to be a life-changing decision. Two events that occurred in close proximity to each other were instrumental in that decision. The first was something my mother said.

I had come home one weekend to see Alicia, my frustrating female nemesis. She was busy that Saturday afternoon, so I found myself with my younger brother Jack and my mother. He was buying a car, and I went with them to the car dealership. At the time I was thinking about becoming a nurse. Male nurses were a rarity and suddenly in big demand. I had a friend at TERROS who was making seven fifty per hour as a male nurse. That was a lot of money at the time. While my brother test-drove a car I told my mother about my plans. I don't know what motivated even that small disclosure to her.

"You'll never make it," she said.

"Why not?" I asked.

"You won't take orders from anybody. Nurses have to take orders from doctors, and you wouldn't like that. You might as well become a doctor. You would probably like ordering people around."

The second event was breaking things off with Alicia once and for all. On that same weekend I spent as much time with Alicia as she would let me. Despite having had many girlfriends and lovers in the two years I had lived away, I still felt a drive to win Alicia's affections.

For reasons that must have made sense at that time I asked her to marry me. It was a desperate act. To my astonishment she didn't display any sign of surprise. She also didn't display any sign of acceptance of my proposal. I left for Phoenix empty-handed and with an empty heart. I had a long talk about Alicia with an older waitress at a Denny's restaurant that night. She was not encouraging.

"I don't think she wants to marry you," she said. "She would have given you a sign that she planned to say yes. There would have been a sign. I believe in signs."

"I don't remember any signs," I said.

Alicia called me a week later and told me to go to hell. My proposal had angered her. She wanted me out of her life. I felt grief-stricken for the entire day. Just one day. The next morning I woke up and realized that a great weight had been lifted off of me. I was done with Alicia.

Whenever I had thought of the future I had always thought Alicia would be part of it. I had never really reflected on what I wanted to do with my life. I experienced a revelation (an uncommon event for me) that I had been dragging her around in my mind for two years without a single indication that she shared any affection for me. The waitress had been correct; I just hadn't seen the signs.

That was the day I decided to become a doctor. It was based on about as much rational thinking as asking Alicia to marry me. It just suddenly seemed like a good idea. For once I felt like I was finally seeing the signs.

Your loving father,
Dad

On The Road

Dear Matt,

When I decided to become a doctor I was living in a nicely converted garage behind an old house in Phoenix. The landlords were a couple in the middle of a divorce. The woman wanted to move into the garage with me, though her husband still lived in the house. It became a sticky situation. I was unusually candid about what a terrible idea that was, and the situation settled down. It was near the end of the semester, and I thought the best thing I could do was move out. I decided to store my stuff, take leave from TERROS, and take a road trip to who-knows-where. I was excited about becoming a doctor but had no clue how to go about getting into medical school.

I applied for in-state residency status in Arizona. That would give me in-state tuition and a shot at the state-supported medical school in Tucson. I had learned that only residents of Arizona were accepted there. I knew I needed to finish my undergraduate degree. To cover my bases I applied to the University of Arizona in Tucson, the University of New Mexico in Albuquerque, and, as a last resort, New Mexico State University in Las Cruces.

I started my trip with little in the way of an agenda. My travels took me as far east as Massachusetts and as far west as the Badlands. Along the way I met my brother Chuck in Washington DC. He was in the air force and had come over from England to attend a huge Christian conference. It was much more engaging than I expected, but I was not the slightest bit interested in converting to Christianity.

I visited relatives in Pennsylvania and actually went to my birthplace, Oregon, Illinois. Oregon felt really creepy. It seemed like the little town was full of nothing but malicious ghosts for me. I saw my relatives and the parents of old friends before hustling out of town as quickly as possible. I visited with the parents of a kid who had been my best friend during childhood. He was living in Dallas. I had a long discussion about religion with his mother that ran into the night. My trip was taking on a strong cosmic theme. In Minneapolis I smoked homegrown dope with a friend of mine from Arizona State. He was dying due to heart failure brought on by muscular dystrophy. I eventually finished my trip on the threshold of an old girlfriend's house back in Phoenix.

"Hi, Chris," I said when she answered the door. "Any chance I could crash with you for a couple of days?"

"You bet," she said with enthusiasm. I had been hoping for a place on the couch, but I began to think I might have a place in the bed. I stayed more than a few days.

The mail that had piled up since my departure was full of bad news. There was a letter stating the denial of my Arizona residency request. With the time I had left, an appeal was out of the question. Perhaps just as bad, the University of New Mexico had lost my entire application package, and I had not been admitted. The University of Arizona would take me but only as an out-of-state student. But I *had* been accepted as an in-state student at New Mexico State University in Las Cruces. There was no time to come up with another option. If I were going to continue as an undergraduate and eventually attend medical school in New Mexico, I would have to move home. Lying in bed one night with Chris, we agreed that this was the worst thing that could have happened to me. But in the end it turned out to be the best turn of events in my life.

Your loving father,
Dad

I'm A Doctor, Damn It

Dear Matt,

I moved home a few days later after saying good-bye to Chris and Phoenix. I'd never move back there. I immediately started looking for work and a place of my own. I was horrified to find myself forced to live at home in my old bedroom for even a couple of weeks. School started and I struck up a relationship with a Mary, a girl I had known years earlier. I started tutoring her in calculus, and within two weeks we were living together in her little house. It was a rocky relationship from the start and only lasted a few intense months.

Life was still melancholy, and being back in Las Cruces didn't help. Following nearly two very positive years of seeing of John Guzman, I was anxious to see another counselor. Like Arizona State, the university offered free counseling. My first appointment was little more than a cursory introduction. Mac Letterman seemed a little cool and not as outgoing as John Guzman. But I had just met him, and I was pretty vague on just what it was that I wanted to do with my bleak view of life. He asked me to complete a MMPI or Minnesota Multiphasic Personality Inventory.

This was my first encounter with this strange and disturbing personality test. Still, I completed the five hundred plus questions and waited for another appointment so we could go through the results. I was pretty uneasy about what a test like that could say about a person like me.

At my second visit I heard all about the MMPI and the theories behind it that indicated my personality traits. The only thing I remember was that the test showed I was anxious. The rest of what Mac said about the test didn't stick very well. It seemed foreign to me and irrelevant to our client-therapist relationship. We made another appointment. I hoped that we could start to establish something a bit chummier.

Having worked as a paramedic at TERROS I was eventually able to land a job as a technician in an emergency department. One night at work I was talking to the cute ward clerk when the radio came to life and the ambulance crew announced that they were en route with a belligerent drunk male with a police escort. Our hearts sank. There was little to do with belligerent drunks except wait for them to sober up or hope that the police would take them. We'd have to wait and see if he was injured, which would mean that he was our problem.

In a flurry much more dramatic than expected, the double doors opened with a mass of police officers and emergency medical technicians struggling with a shouting and extremely agitated man handcuffed to a gurney. The scene was almost comical. I got up to help and joined in the scuffle.

It turned out the man had been driving intoxicated and had plowed through several parked cars before coming to a stop after hitting a telephone pole. As I helped move the man to one of our gurneys and latched the restraints on him, I suddenly recognized him. It was Mac Letterman. He was foaming at the mouth and spitting expletives like a fountain. It was my therapist—drunk, abusive, and disheveled.

Mac had a lot to say that night to everyone who tried to help him. Fortunately he wasn't injured, and his stay was short. As the police walked him back out the door I heard him shout a statement that I recall to this day.

"I'm a doctor, damn it. I help people!"

I canceled my next appointment and didn't seek professional help again for thirteen years.

Your loving father,
Dad

Getting Religion
And Nearly Losing It

Dear Matt,

I became a Christian about two forty-five one rainy morning in January 1975, just a month after the incident with Mac Letterman in the emergency department. My messy conversion was a scene appropriate for a sappy commercial for Christian broadcasting as I slouched down the middle of El Prado Street in the drizzle. My live-in relationship had led to me falling hard for Mary. I thought we had serious long-term potential. She never felt that way. My established pattern of treating women as little more than sex objects was as evident in this relationship as it had been in the past. My life by now was a clutter of short, intense, and one-sided very physical affairs. To my dismay she had asked me to get my own place. I found a little apartment just down the street from our house. After a particularly disturbing theater production one evening that we hardly made it through, we had our big blowup. She felt very much the sex object and discounted my professions of what I called my love for her.

"You've never cared about me as a person." she yelled. "I'm just another conquest to you."

"I love you," I said loudly. "I always have."

"With all my clothes off and waiting for you in bed. Maybe!"

She was right. And as a couple we were over. Down the street I wandered, soaking my brother Bob's borrowed suit and praying to God for help and forgiveness. I felt no bolt of lightning, nor did I feel a lick better, but I've never looked back. I had become a Christian. I felt like what C. S. Lewis described as the most reluctant convert in the kingdom.

Mary and I only lived together for about four months. Two important things did come out of this relationship. One, she taught me to drink bad coffee hot and black. In the mornings she would dump new grounds onto the old grounds in the coffee maker. It perked a terrible brew. But she drank it, and I thought I should drink it. Love does funny things to rational thought.

I once asked why we never had milk or sugar to put in the coffee.

She answered, "You might as well learn to drink it black. When you need cream and sugar the most, you won't have any." These proved to be prophetic words.

The other thing that came out of the affair was my newfound belief, whatever it was, in Jesus. I viewed everything with a new set of eyes. For the first time I began to think in moral terms. There were good things, faith in Jesus for instance, and evil things, like lust and sex outside of marriage. My depressive feelings had not changed, and I started to view them as a sign of lack of faith. I knew very little about the Bible and had only the thinnest grasp on what it really meant to be a Christian. That would take years, and I was anxious to progress in days and weeks. I felt remorse over my previous lifestyle, particularly my time in Phoenix. I wrote evangelical apologies to everyone I thought I had hurt there. The mailing list was mostly female. I attended every prayer group and church service I could find. I felt I was a changed man. When it came to women, though, I often had trouble keeping to my newfound convictions.

I started out in a charismatic form of worship, essentially a modernized version of Pentecostalism. As a result I learned to believe in the supernatural gifts God gave people, including the ability to heal disease, cast out evil spirits, and fight in spiritual warfare with the devil. There was more, and I believed all of it. Despite my best efforts I became involved with young women in the fellowships, and my old habits came back to haunt me. I was even involved briefly with an "unbeliever." These behaviors did not fare me well, and I felt the sting of being "rebuked," or called on the carpet.

I took the criticism to heart and seriously reexamined my relationships with women. For the first time I could see that my history with women was little more than a trail of ruin as a result of my indefensible attitude toward them. I had little capacity for intimacy and a great capacity for sex. I had thoroughly confused the two for years. I may have thought I was a new spiritual being, but I knew plainly that I was vulnerable to falling back into my old ways, as recent experience had displayed. By the end of the spring semester I was finally getting over Mary but not out of the woods with women in general. I thought I needed a plan for the summer before I got into trouble again.

One day in the student newspaper there was an ad calling for volunteers to work two seasons on an archeological dig in Israel starting in May. I thought God had spoken. I would go to the dig and be out of the company of women for the entire summer. I could "get my head together."

The dig proved to be my first real challenge as a charismatic Christian. I worked with nearly one hundred seminary students who were much smarter about their beliefs than I was, but in my mind they were sadly lacking any true faith. I fought and argued for the entire summer, trying hard to cling to what I felt were my superior spiritual beliefs. I failed. As the second season of the dig wound up, I found myself sharing my faith with a small group who clung to a more basic and solid Christianity: a struggling former Jew from Yale, a lesbian from Milwaukee, and a reformed alcoholic Baptist from the West Coast. He always wore a big "Praise the Lord" button on his hat. Everyone in the dig just called him "Praise the Lord" in derision, and few knew his name. I had given up on the many spiritual gifts I thought I possessed and struggled with much of what I had learned as a charismatic. What was left was a new Christian just beginning a walk of faith.

I returned home humbled and convinced that what I had accepted unquestioningly as truth was in fact a package of bad theology. I had given up women when I left town; now I wondered if I should add charismatics to the same list.

Your loving father,
Dad

Me in Israel during the summer of 1975

The Last Quiet Years

Dear Matt,

Bipolar disorder often starts with depression and is then dormant for years until the twenties. That was my pattern. Much happened during those quiet years. After I came back from Israel, having sworn off women and charismatic Christians, I met your mom: a woman and a charismatic Christian. Ten weeks later we were engaged. I hadn't planned on falling in love again. She was a beautiful and bright woman, and I fell head over heels for her at our first meeting. We met by the copier one night on the third floor of Branson Hall Library, where she worked. She walked by with a pile of books and said hello. I turned around and heard bells. Who was this girl, and how did I keep her talking so I could find out? I talked stupid trash just to keep her standing there. I never offered to hold the books, and she didn't move on until I realized I knew someone who knew who she was: my younger brother.

I woke my brother Jack up at 10:30 PM and peppered him with questions about this girl. He knew her name and where she met a friend at lunch to study the Bible. My brother, I later learned, harbored romantic dreams for this same girl

"You aren't thinking about asking her out, are you?" he asked sleepily.

It was nearly midnight, I was pestering him about this girl, and he thought I wasn't interested in her?

"No," I lied.

I was at the proper place at lunch the next day. My brother was hurrying down the sidewalk to the same patch of grass. Your future mother enthusiastically accepted my offer of a date to a ministry program on Saturday night. The ministry was for street people and operated out of an old converted bar called the Green Frog.

Suddenly I remembered that I was committed to taking a group of high school kids hiking through the Grand Canyon that weekend. I couldn't take your mother out on the date. My brother excitedly offered to take my place. I was horrified. Her enthusiasm for our Saturday night date didn't give her any easy way out of going on the date with my brother. So I hiked the Grand Canyon that weekend with one thing on my mind, and it wasn't the stellar beauty of the country I was in; it was "the girl" going out with my little brother. That date proved to be his one shot. Your mom and I started going out later, and she never dated another man. She had been dating four guys at the time we met. We just celebrated the thirty-second anniversary of our first date: November 6, 1975. In the big scheme of things, meeting and marrying your mom makes all that followed in the next few years appear almost trivial.

Medical school is the subject of a whole other story. I survived its rigors and even flourished in many ways. My bipolar disorder didn't rear its ugly head until the end of my senior year. You were a year old. By that time your mom and I had been married nearly five years and were totally unprepared for what was about to happen to us.

Your loving father,

Dad

This is a photograph of your mother taken by your Uncle Jack in the fall of 1975. Used with permission

The House On
Constitution Street

Dear Matt,

The second half of bipolar disorder, mania, started out in very subtle ways for me. In the spring of 1981 I was 27, and it seemed like I had just gotten a really bad idea into my head and couldn't be talked out of it. I had a big plan to buy a house. In every regard it was a lousy plan. We lived with you in a cozy little mobile home in Albuquerque that was more than adequate for our needs. The first problem was that we couldn't possibly afford to buy a house. My salary as an intern was just over fifteen thousand dollars. We had no savings and no down payment. Selling the mobile home would be difficult at that time and would generate little cash. I was thoroughly convinced, however, that we had to buy a house from a friend of ours. The idea was a grandiose bipolar thought that became an obsession. Grandiose thoughts are very difficult to argue with when their origin is mania. Your mom did her best.

I was very irritable when I faced any opposition to my plan, which was everywhere. I developed a convoluted scheme to generate a down payment from relatives and even got the owners to finance part of the purchase. Our lender was reluctant to offer us a mortgage. I badgered the loan officer mercilessly and shamelessly. The math was against me. The only ace in my hand was my MD degree and the certainty of future income. Your mom was exhausted trying to convince me that we could be very comfortable on my income in the trailer and that we could be very house-poor in the little house I wanted to buy on Constitution Street. I could not be swayed, and I worked day and night on my crazy notion.

Anyone who saw this as bipolar mania would have had to be a very insightful person. It looked like simply the harebrained scheme of an obsessive person. Only in retrospect did we see this as the beginning of my first manic episode. Symptoms such as anxiety, sleeplessness, increased energy, and depressed mood were just down the road for me. It would never have occurred to me to see a professional about my great idea. It was, as far as I was concerned, a very reasonable course. Grandiose bipolar thinking is like that. It always seems reasonable to the person doing the thinking.

Ultimately your mother deferred to my judgment, something she eventually learned not to do. She never liked the idea and never really liked the house. We were comfortable but poor because of the house. In the years to come, large, expensive ideas would be a consistent feature of my illness. You know about manic schemes—you participated in a few of them. You certainly played a role in buying a luxury car one year. We would sail together years later on a boat that started out as another bipolar idea.

Your loving father,
Dad

Our family in the front yard of the house on
Constitution Street during the fall of 1981

Panic In The Pediatric Clinic

Dear Matt,

The joy of graduating from the University of New Mexico School of Medicine hadn't even begun to tarnish when I started my internship in July 1981. We were in our new house on Constitution Street by then. You were almost one. There are many theories about the triggers of bipolar symptoms. One of them is that an unusually stressful event can bring them on. I think sooner or later they will come, and a stressful situation only hurries the process. That seems to be what happened to me. I was already mildly manic after the home-buying splurge, but the symptoms were masked in the mayhem that the internship introduced to my life. Suddenly I was expected to act like a real doctor. All interns faced the stress of trying to take four years of medical school knowledge and applying it to real patients. We all had heads full of knowledge and very few practical skills or experience. Stress doesn't start to describe the process.

In the fall I started working in the pediatric clinic at the Bernalillo County Medical Center, taking care of every kind of ill child you can imagine. Fear had characterized my life experiences as an intern up to that point. I learned what real fear was like in that clinic. We offered many types of medical specialty services during the day: neurology, cardiology, endocrinology, and even dysmorphology. The care of these patients was part of the daily routine of the interns. It was mind-boggling and really rarely routine. The worst part was night call. Once the clinic closed the intern on call was responsible for all the urgent and emergency pediatric patients that walked in or were carried in. That was a lot of patients, and they had a variety of problems that challenged even the most senior of staff. The senior staff went home at five. The more junior staff just disappeared into the hospital. All that was left were interns.

My first night on call started with a busy and at times confounding day. I was anxious at the prospect of being alone in the clinic all night. I soon learned what a voluminous capacity for anxiety I actually had. Shortly after the clinic closed the resident from the pediatric hospital ward came down to visit me. A resident was a second- or third-year trainee who had already completed his or her internship in pediatrics and was considerably more experienced and skilled. He or she was responsible for all the patients in the clinic who were too complicated for the intern and for all the children who required admission to the hospital. That night the resident had strong opinions on both these responsibilities. He did not wish to carry out either of them. I was to leave him alone. He wanted no requests for consultations and no admissions. I was shocked, and worse, I believed him. I soon learned that this was standard intern intimidation and that he was powerless to refuse my requests, but at that time I thought the voice of God had spoken.

The evening did not start well, and it deteriorated quickly. My first patient was an infant from the cardiology clinic with some type of heart defect and a murmur. She had a temperature of 104 degrees. I knew this was very high, but I didn't know what I was supposed to do about it. I examined the irritable baby and found nothing. I couldn't hear the murmur that the parents said was as loud as a steam engine. I left the room to think. I had just enough time to get a cup of tea warmed up before the next patient arrived.

The second patient of the evening was a six-year-old girl with a respiratory infection who had developed a massively swollen, red, hot, and painful right knee. The knee looked like it had been beaten with a bat and sprayed with brick-colored paint. I had never seen a joint so big and hot. But then I had seen very few things at that point in my training. I briefly examined the girl's knee and stepped back out of the room to my tea. My measure of anxiety was growing by the second. I was completely at a loss but felt that I needed to sort these problems out without assistance. That was a foolish feeling. It was a dangerous feeling.

I thought I was at my limit and was paralyzed. Then the secretary came into the clinic area.

"The microcephalic with seizures is on her way up from emergency. I'm getting the chart," she said.

She might as well have told me that a meteorite was going to strike the clinic in thirty seconds. I had no idea what I would do. A microcephalic child was a baby born essentially without a brain. He or she had just enough brain tissue to breathe and keep the heart beating. They looked like little Neanderthals with small foreheads and no skulls behind them. They didn't live long. I had one coming up the stairs having seizures.

I entertained the idea of just walking out of the clinic. I couldn't scream. I had to call for help. It dawned on me that I could call someone other than the pediatric resident to look at the hot knee: the orthopedic resident. He was much more likely to be interested in a good case like that than the pediatric resident. I paged him and waited. I was surprised to notice that I was drenched in sweat. The microcephalic baby arrived in her teenage mother's arms, and the secretary put them in a room. My heart was pounding.

The orthopedic resident called back. He was gruff at first but quickly warmed up at the description of the knee. He thought I knew what the problem was. I knew no such thing. He and his team would be at the clinic shortly. And they were.

I went to see the microcephalic baby. Her mother was in tears.

"I'm sorry," she said. "I just forgot to give her the medicines, and she had another seizure. She seems okay now."

I was flooded with relief. "What medications is she on?" I asked.

The young mother produced several small bottles of liquids. It was not a simple regimen; that much I could tell. I read each label. I didn't recognize a single drug. "It must be hard to keep up with all these medicines," I said.

"I just forget," she said in her tears. She held her baby closely.

"I think you're doing the right thing here. You just have to remember to give her all of her medicines on time. She'll be okay," I said. Although what I said was correct, I felt like I was bluffing.

The mother was comforted, and she packed up her medications and left. The parents of the fevered infant were peeking out of the door. I had no choice. My fear incapacitated me until the secretary pushed the issue.

"Don't worry about that jerk resident. He gives every intern the same sad tale of being overworked on the ward and to not bother him. That baby is really sick, and he's going to have to admit her," she said.

I called the pediatric resident.

"Look," I said. "I've seen a kid with a septic joint, a microcephalic with seizures, and still have a febrile infant here. I need you to come down and look at this baby."

He didn't argue with me. He knew immediately that the infant needed to be evaluated and admitted. Up until then I hadn't realized that a resident physician couldn't ignore my request.

I was done. I had actually done a good job. I recognized serious problems and gotten them into the right hands. I had handled the more routine problem of the baby having seizures. As an intern I should have been greatly relieved. The orthopedic team was having a great time looking at the knee with visions of sticking a huge needle into it. The grumpy pediatric team came down to see the baby with the fever. Soon the clinic was empty and locked up. I went to the on-call room to sit by the phone and wait for my next duty. I never closed my eyes. I couldn't stop the feelings of panic.

Your loving father,
Dad

And What Happened After That

Dear Matt,

Weeks passed after the pediatric clinic night, and I could not settle down. I was living in a state of near panic, with anxiety served at breakfast, lunch, and dinner. This caused horrible nervousness, chest palpitations, and trouble catching my breath. I was distracted. I didn't sleep much. I didn't seem to need it. Whenever the opportunity presented itself I would skip out of the specialty clinics and drink herbal tea somewhere safe. Herbal tea was my comfort at the time. I can't stand it now. I was quick to cry and irritable and drank beer every evening that I was home. Your mom was worried. Everything in my life seemed to take a backseat to my anxiety and fear.

This was to be the next form that bipolar disorder took for me. Some features, like intense, relentless anxiety, would be prominent for the rest of my life. We assumed, incorrectly, that I was just frightened of being an intern. I *was* frightened of being an intern, even though I was rapidly developing prowess and actually having some positive experiences.

It is hard to articulate what those first few months of mania were like. I had finally started my new life with bipolar disorder. Anxiety and constant worry were predominant. Nothing is more mind occupying than anxiety. I felt as though at any moment something terrible was going to happen. But there wasn't anything terrible about to happen. As an intern I was exposed to many things that made me anxious, and they just leapt onto the hog pile of nervousness I was already experiencing. No one expected life to be easy for an intern. Most interns managed their anxiety without much difficulty, taking each day in stride, but I was well past that point. I was irritable and depressed.

I began to develop plans to get out of my situation as an intern, because I was convinced that was my problem. It just seemed impossible that there wasn't an external cause that would explain all of my symptoms. I couldn't understand how every other intern seemed to handle the stresses so well. I began crying at odd times and in response to minor things. A sad chapter in a novel I was reading made me bawl all the way through the bus ride to the hospital one morning. I would hide in the bathroom. One thing I didn't understand was that when called upon my mind seemed sharp and focused on my work. I had energy. Sleep came with difficulty despite the exhausting days and nights. I felt as though I was in a whirligig of fast thinking and activity with a depressed and anxious mood. If I wasn't crazy already, I was going to go crazy feeling like this.

One of my professors noticed the changes in me. He supervised our family medicine clinic. He decided to take action, much like Frank Johnson years earlier. One afternoon he called the clinic and insisted I be sent to his office immediately. No one argued with him, and my patient appointments for the afternoon were cancelled. In the office he seemed surprisingly chatty and friendly. If I was in any sort of trouble you couldn't have told it from his demeanor. Soon he asked how I was doing.

"Not too well. I'm just feeling stressed all the time. Working at night is hard. You remember being an intern. I can't get enough sleep." I didn't tell him I never slept much anyway.

"Are you going to make it okay?" he asked pointedly.

"I'm okay." I wasn't ready to tell anyone what was really going on. I could hardly explain it to your mom. I still blamed everything on just being an intern. "I'm just feeling pretty worn out."

"You're an intern; you ought to feel stress. You just seem to be coping poorly," he said. "I don't want to see you flip out too." A pediatric intern had recently locked himself in a bathroom for hours and refused to come out. He was off duty and in counseling. I needed to be in that same situation.

We talked for a while longer, and he surprised me again. He had arranged for me to have the rest of the afternoon off. He *gave* me an afternoon off. This was unprecedented for any intern.

I hurried home, where your pregnant mom was busy wrestling with you. My professor pulled off this trick twice more. No one caught on that he was doing his little part to keep me going. Few professors would have noticed my problems, and fewer still would have acted as he had to do something about them. My fellow interns assumed I was in some kind of trouble every time he called. I did nothing to dispel that notion.

Once again a single person had made an effort to help me. At best it was a temporary fix that let me go home and feel terrible. That was better than feeling terrible roaming a hospital. What I didn't understand was why I didn't feel better getting away from my internship even for half a day. I still blamed my feelings on my position as an intern and clung to that mistaken conclusion for the rest of the year.

Your loving father,
Dad

The End Of Internship

Dear Matt,

I was a good intern. I learned quickly, and at the times when it really mattered I had a lot of focus. I was well liked. They loved me in the emergency department, and I enjoyed being there. Something about the pace and intensity drew my attention and concentration. I would feel a little better when I was so distracted. Late in my internship I had gained confidence and competence. I wasn't the same person who had started out the previous summer. I was easily persuaded that I belonged in emergency medicine, and I thought that I could kiss this terrible time of anxiety and fear good-bye once I was done with my family medicine internship. I resigned from my residency effective at the end of my internship and started looking for emergency medicine positions. I gave some excuse for leaving. I didn't know the truth; I didn't even know a good lie.

I did my last intern rotations without a problem. Ryan was born in the middle of one of my last shifts as an intern. I left early and made it home and to another hospital on gasoline vapors. Ryan was born the next morning. I was back to being an intern the next day. Two weeks later I finished my final shift as an intern at midnight. The new interns were coming into the hospital dressed neatly, their white jacket pockets bulging with pocket guides and notebooks.

We, the interns of 1981–82, went outside and started passing around two bottles of champagne as we sat on the curb. There must have been a dozen of us. We looked like weary veterans dressed in scrubs and half shaven. We waved to the new interns and pointed to the doors. We no longer carried clinical manuals or notebooks. Most of us carried just pens and stethoscopes. I felt elated during those few minutes outside the emergency room doors. I'll always remember those moments. I was done with the toughest year of my life up until that point, and I had done better than just survive. I felt I was leaving on a high point. My anxiety would be behind me. It looked like I could work full-time in emergency medicine. The bottle came by again. I liked champagne. I walked out to my old Volkswagen feeling fuzzy and glad.

I wanted to go home to Las Cruces. Given how I felt about my life, the old hometown looked pretty attractive. I don't know if I'd ever felt that way before. I'd been away five years and had a family of four. I felt certain that being back in familiar surroundings would stop my depressed and anxious mood. And I would no longer be an intern. I was confident I could do the work of an emergency physician.

Fortunately the medical group that had the contract for the emergency room in Las Cruces needed another person. I was hired part-time. I found other part-time work covering rural emergency departments. At first we stayed in Albuquerque while I started work. We put the house on the market to sell. A new life, I hoped, was beginning. I don't need to tell you how wrong I was.

Your loving father,
Dad

Déjà Vu: My First Year Of Practice

Dear Matt,

The high point of ending internship was short-lived. I just took all of my problems with me in the moving truck. I took a big box marked "bipolar disorder" right along with the beds and the other boxes.

Shortly after moving to Las Cruces I found the old adobe house we lived in for the next three years. It seemed affordable to me. It was small but unique with two-feet-thick walls. Even though we hadn't sold the house in Albuquerque, I insisted that we buy this house. I was certain I could generate the money, though none of my new positions paid very well. It was the same story as the last house. I was feeling confident, and the costs appeared to me to be no problem. We ended up losing our shirt on the first house and selling it for less than we owed. We struggled with two house payments for months, and even after selling the house we had payments to make to resolve the debt we still carried. This was the second time I had dumped us into financial trouble over my grand ideas.

I started in the emergency departments. In no time I was overwhelmed with the old anxiety and sleeplessness. I was constantly demanding sex from your mother. I started drinking again every evening after work or on my nights off, looking for a way to stop the relentless anxiety. Funny thing was, I was at my best at work when the pace and demands kept me focused on practicing medicine. I started traveling to do shifts in other towns.

I did well everywhere but didn't feel well. I was again convinced that the very demands of my work were causing my symptoms. I began having trouble leaving the house to go to work. I gave up on herbal tea and switched to coffee. You can imagine how puzzled we were. I was doing what I thought had been the right thing to keep my emotional keel level. It hadn't worked. Again I started trying to find a way out of this anxiety. I felt trapped. The first year of practice was looking like the internship I had struggled through the year before. I experienced the same anxiety, the same panic, and the same sense that I couldn't escape my emotions or my work. And just like I had done as an intern, I blamed my symptoms on my work and not on my own mental function.

A small disaster struck in January. I severely injured my back and made the living room floor my living quarters. The water bed was too painful to reach and too painful to try to sleep in. A week later I developed pneumonia. Being newly self-employed, I had no insurance, no income, and no savings. We had been living on the edge of debt and income. I'd never been so sick in my life. Moving around on my hands and knees took my breath away. I couldn't stop the chills and sweats. My anxiety was better because I was too sick to be moody. I was just frightened about how we were going to make it without a paycheck. The lack of anxiety and my other symptoms helped convince me, again, that my work was behind my problems.

While in this condition I received an offer to return to the University of New Mexico and complete a one-year fellowship in emergency medicine. To me it was the ticket out of my moody misery. I was convinced that if I was just a little smarter and more confident about my work I could better control my anxiety. The fellowship was going to be my big escape. But it was just another boat without oars.

Your loving father,
Dad

Emergency room entrance, Roswell, New Mexico, in 1982

The Fellowship That I
Thought Would Save Me

Dear Matt,

When you turned three, Ryan was one, and we were broke. It was 1983. I had accepted the fellowship at the University of New Mexico. It seemed like another good idea that would help stop my bipolar symptoms. We moved back to Albuquerque, renting a house on Vassar Street near the law school. I needed to keep all of my part-time emergency department positions in Las Cruces for the income. By now not only was I plagued with relentless anxiety and sleeplessness, I picked up what appeared to be boundless energy. Mania was strengthening its grip on me. During my fellowship I would work five days in the emergency department at the university. On weekends I would drive two hundred miles south or east and work day and night in my old emergency departments. I'd drive back in the dark on Sunday and repeat the routine week after week. I bought an old Chevy pickup truck for the commute. No one noticed my remarkable lack of sleep and the terrific energy needed to keep up this schedule. I was finally enjoying some of the benefits, so to speak, of mania. The year went well. Just eleven days after it ended Callie was born.

Your mother managed pregnancy, childbirth, and child rearing as if she had earned a PhD in the field. This was a good thing, because I was largely absent in mind, if not in body, so much of the time.

She carried on through my travails with babies in her arms or her tummy, or frequently both. She took our frequent moves in style. Her stability through these early tough times was just a hint of what she would be like when things worsened over the years.

I finished the fellowship year with new confidence, a certificate, and three publications. I felt better about my field and my abilities. It was a strange time for me. Plagued by anxiety, I had developed the ability to feel free of excessive worry and fear while seeing patients. My manic thinking and activity helped me overcome my depressed and anxious mood. Work took on greater importance to me. Paradoxically, I feared work when I was away from it but felt best when I was in the emergency department. As much as I prospered at work, I floundered at home. I had no tools to control my moods and my anxiety while away from work. I did my best with what I had left to bring home to you kids after work. It wasn't much.

By this time I was only working in two emergency departments. I worked days and nights, weekends and holidays. My schedule had no pattern, and my ability to live on little sleep was an asset. I tried hard to keep some kind of routine, but it was impossible to maintain. Some days the most I could do was drink coffee and move the sprinkler around the yard. This lack of any circadian rhythm was probably aggravating my symptoms. It didn't matter if I was at work or home—I *felt* the same. Life was a blur of lousy symptoms. Because I didn't know I was bipolar I didn't realize how poorly people with bipolar disorder tolerated a lack of routine.

My bipolar symptoms persisted the entire time I practiced emergency medicine. Looking back, I have no idea how I tolerated them and never thought to seek help. Days away from work were worse than days at work at times. I needed the distraction. It wasn't enough to have a loving wife and a great family.

After five years of practice our emergency medicine group gave up the contracts to the hospitals I worked in. That was fine with me; I was ready to quit emergency medicine. I started working on a solo practice idea I had hatched earlier in the year. It would turn out to be my one really great manic plan. As had been the case so often, I thought that having more control in my life would help to quell my symptoms. I foolishly imagined that a solo medical practice would give me better control of my life. I was wrong on both counts.

Your loving father,
Dad

Into The Abyss

Dear Matt,

You had started elementary school by the time I ventured into private practice in 1987. I don't really remember much about that time in your life other than your first day of school. I cried. My mental issues dominated every aspect of my life by then. We had moved into a new house the year before you started school. We could barely afford it, but I was optimistic about my professional future.

The grandest of my many grand ideas ever was my solo medical practice. Not only was I going to try my hand at solo practice, I was going to open up a type of practice completely new to Las Cruces: occupational medicine. A saner man would have shuddered at the magnitude of the risk I was taking. I had no clear idea of the need for occupational medical care in Las Cruces, much less how much it would cost to set up and run. I began working on the idea before our group left the hospital and stayed on with the new medical group long enough to start my private practice.

I hired a consultant to help me set up the practice, order equipment, and plan staffing. His only experience had been setting up a specialist's practice. That had proven to be an inexpensive practice to operate and required very little in the way of space, equipment, or working capital. It made money right away. A friend had started a private pediatric practice about the same time and was making money from the beginning. My loan officer's only experience with setting up medical practices was loaning money to my friend. So I had two inexperienced consultants who had no idea of the magnitude of what I was doing and the ambitiousness of my plans. The mistakes made at the beginning nearly crippled the practice in its early months.

To be adequately prepared for the broad range of patients seen in occupational medicine I needed many large and expensive pieces of equipment, most notably an x-ray machine. While I could have done well with a small single-phase unit, I leased a cutting-edge three-phase machine from my consultant's husband that cost three times as much. Altogether I borrowed money for over a hundred and eighty thousand dollars in equipment and setup costs. I hired friends to staff the clinic. They were highly qualified nurses and technicians. I rented and remodeled expensive office space. My plans knew no bounds, and I was utterly confident of my success. I took large draws of money from our working capital loan to live on while the practice was being set up.

This was a classic manic scheme: a huge undertaking made without adequate forethought and little concern for the cost or risks involved. The whole project required supreme confidence. It also required at least some business sense, something I was entirely lacking. As a rational person would have predicted, the whole thing was a house of cards that quickly collapsed under the weight of high-priced and short-term loans, staggering expenses, and no patients. The practice opened a month late and to a whimper. My first patient was a cut finger that arrived during our open house party. He was an employee of a friend, and I gladly stitched him up. I would not see another patient for weeks.

The mess I had created did not immediately alarm me. My confidence was overwhelming. However, as the weeks went by with no income and a steady outflow of salaries, rent, and new loan payments, my anxiety built all over again. I started marketing my practice the best I could. My loan officer began to worry. He had expected an immediate cash income. My projections, which I had worked on day and often all night, projected generous income and profit long before that time. I realized I was building debt that was going to approach a quarter of a million dollars. My normal anxiety turned to panic. I was soon receiving ominous messages from my bank, and I began to try negotiating a better lease. I worked feverishly at my spreadsheets, trying to force the practice into life by my will.

As has repeatedly proven to be the case in my life with bipolar disorder, the right person came along at the right time. A friend introduced me to another banker, one with years of experience in helping failing banks and businesses. He looked over my numbers and immediately concluded that his bank wouldn't touch me. Although he had no prospect of making money from me, he was willing to help. In the evenings we pored over my spreadsheets using his coffee table. He had no difficulty finding the obvious major source of my problem: my practice was far too expensive to ever pay for itself. I had created high fixed expenses like the x-ray machine, but I had hired a large staff with high salaries as well. Every one of my clinical staff had to go. I needed a barebones crew if I had any hope of pulling out. He was not optimistic.

I reluctantly faced reality. I fired my friends, who promptly ceased to be friends. They had placed their confidence in a bipolar individual who could not deliver on his promises. I begged my landlord for a break and implored my banker to lighten my payment burden. The bank's response was to cut off any further loans. I had to cut my salary significantly.

While this was happening the practice was starting to show some promising life. Somehow the word had finally gotten out, and I was having fewer and fewer days without patients. My machines were starting to generate charges, and we were starting to see income. The draconian measures that the newfound banker had put in place lowered the cost of business so far that I paid all of my monthly bills for the first time seven months after starting. I made a profit two months later. The weight of my debt was considerable, but the practice began to show itself as a potentially viable business.

I was really crazy by then. In my mania I had created a monster. Like it or not, I was now stuck with my baby, and it was a hungry one. I was back in the pits of anxiety and fear. I really had something to be afraid of: failure. That just threw the proverbial fuel on the fire of my raging moods. I rarely slept and often crunched my financial numbers all night. I was irritable and a sexual fanatic despite my moods. I watched every penny that came or went from the practice and sat for hours at Hiebert's, my favorite coffee shop, swilling coffee and thinking. I saw patients as late as needed. I could talk nonstop for hours, and patient visits were long. I was intensely focused on work and my patients and thrilled with each and every one I saw. I loved the patient care. I was scared to death of the business aspects. I was so distracted that my involvement at home suffered even further. It reached the point where the only time I was comfortable was when I was seeing a patient. With them I was comfortable finally being a physician again and not a businessman.

You remember the practice. I worked lots of evenings and nights, and you guys would come down and play in the office. The building had a long dark hallway that appeared to have no end away from the lights of my office. Your favorite games were jacking the candy machine and racing down that dark hallway at breakneck speed on the wheeled exam chairs. I had been jacking the big money machine and was now hurtling down a long dark hallway with no idea what the end would be.

Your loving father,
Dad

Me hosting the grand opening of my medical practice in 1987

Photograph courtesy of Jack Diven

Meeting My First Psychiatrist

Dear Matt,

Just when I thought I was through the financial crisis of the practice, two things happened. My closest colleague's son drowned in their hot tub. You knew him. His mother called me as the ambulance picked him up and asked me to meet them in the emergency department. I did. He was dead on arrival, but I did everything I could to save him. My colleague had just started in a new practice in a different city. I called him with the news.

Oddly, it was a much more trivial incident that finally pushed me over the edge. I received a complaint by phone from an employer who was unhappy about the size of my bill for treating one of their employees. The charges were reasonable, but my reaction was not. I was suddenly gripped with all the panic I could muster. Suddenly I was certain all the gains the practice had made would evaporate. I was lost in a disaster of my own making. The complaints would pile up, and no one would send me another patient. None of this happened. I was just creating a catastrophe from a simple problem. The call from the employer set off a terrific emotional response that was hardly rational. Still, I told my secretary that we needed to review every charge on our fee schedule and to call this complaining employer and work out a better arrangement. I left the clinic.

I don't know if I had patients waiting or not. Usually I would not miss any patient. I needed every dollar of income I could generate. I ate a hamburger alone at a spot where I could get an overview of town and wondered what to do. One small complaint had set off a Krakatoa-sized reaction.

I went to the hospital to pick up x-ray and consultation reports from patients I referred there. Since the incident with my friend's son, even going to the hospital caused me anxiety, and I rarely went there anymore. In the hall I literally ran into Dr. White. He was a friend and colleague and most importantly a psychiatrist. I blurted out a head full of what was on my mind right then and there. I cared nothing for privacy. He was taken aback a bit by this outburst but quietly asked me if I could come by his office at 5:00 PM to continue our conversation. I was hugely relieved. I even went back to work. I don't know why I was so relieved. Up until that time I had never given a thought to asking someone for professional help. I was a doctor, damn it.

I was at Dr. White's office well before five o'clock. He opened the door on time, and we spent more than an hour of his evening going over everything I could think of. It was as if the cork had popped out of the rotted champagne bottle. My speech was pressured, and I really didn't know what to focus on. He didn't say much about what he thought was going on, but he suggested I would benefit from an antidepressant. I would have taken cyanide if he had recommended it.

I'd been taking sample medications out of my closet trying to control my symptoms, and I wondered if he had anything better than those. Antidepressants were difficult drugs to take in those days because they were loaded with tiresome side effects. But I don't think I cared. I was ready for anything that could take the anxiety and depression away.

We met weekly after that. He tried several different additional medications, mostly anti-anxiety drugs, but they didn't help. Finally he tried a long-acting anti-anxiety drug that tended to be mood stabilizing, which seemed to be beneficial. Without knowing it, or at least not telling me, he had placed me on a simple regimen for bipolar disorder. He had started a mood stabilizer to control mania and an antidepressant to control depression. The medicines helped. I enjoyed talking to him.

Dr. White was the kind of psychiatrist who did psychotherapy and let his patients do most of the talking. He let me blab away. Over time he started asking about dreams and my past. We dug into some dark territory of my growing up that I rarely gave thought to and much that I didn't immediately care to remember. I kept waiting for the morning when I'd say just the right thing and everything would be better. He called that the "Aha!" experience. But talking didn't do much to improve me; it just helped me understand myself much better. Understanding doesn't stop bipolar disorder. I think that is why Dr. White tried the series of medications.

The timing of seeing Dr. White was fortuitous. My disorder deteriorated substantially during the three years I saw him, and he was available to try to manage it. My practice and money worries improved markedly late in 1987. I would start in the mornings and see patients until late in the evening. My energy was almost boundless. I slept a couple hours a night if I needed to. Even with my situational improvement I had no real change in my symptoms aside from the effect of the medications. I still clung to the belief that my circumstances drove my symptoms, particularly after our close call with financial collapse. I didn't know what to do but stick with my situation, and I placed a great deal of hope in Dr. White. That faith was not ill placed.

Your loving father,
Dad

The World At War

Dear Matt,

During my years in emergency medicine I started working as the medical director for the local ambulance service. That was an ill-defined job before there was much regulation of emergency medical services. I continued this position during my days in private practice. At that time medical directing was interesting work, but it was mostly paper shuffling, protocol writing, and quality assurance. The service was evolving into providing advanced life support, something new to our county.

In 1988, when you were eight, you and I went to one of the first meetings of the National Association of Emergency Medical Service Physicians in San Francisco. I met the medical directors of several cities. One in particular described how he had made an impact on patient care by driving an old police car with a radio and emergency lights and siren to emergency scenes. He enjoyed it and learned a great deal more about his system than he ever learned by reading reports. That gave me the bug to try the same thing. I soon learned, once I got the hang of it, that attending emergency scenes was the best way to observe the quality of care the paramedics were delivering.

When I got back I ordered a little emergency light that went on my dashboard and borrowed a radio from the ambulance service. One evening I went out to try to go to an emergency involving a motorcycle wreck. I plugged in my light and off I went, bugging through intersections somewhat recklessly. I got lost. The police found me, and

I was pulled over.

"Oh," the officer said. "It's just you."

"I was looking for the motorcycle wreck, but I can't find it," I said.

The police were watching my end of town for a drunken guy with a small red dash light who was pulling people over and pretending to be a police officer. They had thought they had caught him. I spoke later with the chief of police, and he recommended that I get a complete roof-mounted emergency light bar and siren. I applied for an emergency vehicle permit and with that purchased all the equipment. I was soon spending many an evening and weekend running around the county to emergency scenes. I occasionally went out on calls over my lunch hour. You guys would sometimes go with me in the evening or on weekends and help operate the emergency lights and siren.

My mental status was changing during this time. Bipolar disorder may cause chaotic thinking in some ways but very goal-oriented focus in other ways. I was very focused on my work. My speeding mind easily welcomed the excitement of racing around town with lights flashing and siren blaring.

But despite the additional exhilaration I was enjoying, my moods were deteriorating. A new feature popped into my mind: paranoia. It appeared suddenly. I have no recall of any incident that triggered it. It really just showed up in my consciousness without warning. Unfortunately I was frightened at times of people I had to work with. At first the focus was the police department. Later it included my own paramedics. Ultimately I was afraid of Nazis and Chinese agents. It sounds ridiculous now, but during the paranoia it felt real and frightening. I tried to overcome it by continuing to do what I always did with the ambulance service.

I recall a particularly troubling event during that period. One evening your mom and I were watching *The World at War* with Robert Mitchum. It involved Nazis, and I really had trouble sitting through it. I was afraid of being gassed by Nazis. I heard a call on my radio monitor for a motor vehicle collision near our house, and I decided to go to it. I left your mom and you guys and raced down the street to the scene. It was a chilly early spring night in 1989.

The accident was a minor rear end collision with a lot more

complaining than apparent injury. I usually took pictures but didn't this time and went to talk with the ambulance supervisor. She was bored. The police shift supervisor joined us. He was bored. I was suddenly alert to the fact that more than the necessary number of police cars were pulling up. It didn't occur to me that no one had anything else to do that night. What did occur to me was that the police were probably preparing to capture me. I feared that the supervisor's small talk was intended to keep me standing around until they had enough officers to take me down. I hurried away.

I had to walk by a few police cars and officers to get to my vehicle. Everyone seemed to be looking at me. I pulled away as another police car pulled in behind me. At May Street I shut down not only my emergency lights but also my headlights. I watched to see if any of the police cars followed me. I turned down different side streets, using the manual transmission to slow down without using my brakes and giving my position away with brake lights. I was actually scared. An officer could be waiting for me at any turn. In case the police had gone by my house looking for me, I crossed several neighborhoods that I knew had winding streets and good visibility before I turned for home. I eventually reached the house. No one was in the street. I slipped under the streetlight and into the garage. I had to brake, but I thought I was safe by then. It had taken an hour to get home from a scene that had been just blocks away.

Your mom was reading by then, and you guys were all in bed. She asked how the accident went, and I told her it was just a minor collision.

"It sure took you a long time," she said. "Did you go on another call?"

"I had to take my time coming home," I said nonchalantly. "I had to dodge the police again. I think they really meant to get me tonight." This was all news to her.

"The police were after you? Why?" She sounded alarmed. "Have you done something?"

"No, they're after me for some reason. I don't understand it myself. They have lots of opportunities, but they seem to be looking for just the right one, and I thought tonight was going to be it." I hung up my jacket and turned off the radio. I don't think I noticed that I had upset your mom at that point. In fact, I was so casual about being chased by the police that I think I upset her considerably.

"Are you certain you've done nothing wrong?" she kept asking.

I couldn't convince her it was just a conspiracy of some kind. I told her about the Nazis being in on it. She got really quiet.

"You don't think this is all a little strange? I mean, a conspiracy to capture you that involves the police and Nazis?" she asked in an excessively calm voice.

"It is strange, all right. I don't get it. But I think if I'm careful they won't get me. Scares me a bit though, especially at scenes like this one," I answered.

"Have you told Dr. White about being followed?"

"I can if you want me to. It hasn't come up," I said.

"I'd like that," your mom said.

This was the beginning of some bad times for us.

Your loving father,
Dad

Me at the scene of a motor vehicle accident in 1985

Photograph courtesy of William P. Diven

The White Rabbit

Dear Matt,

If Dr. White thought my conspiracy theories were interesting, I must have really piqued his interest a couple months later when I told him I was hearing voices. I seemed to be headed in the wrong direction mentally. I was having nightmares of being gassed by Nazis. My sleep, which was infrequent and fragmented, seemed to have all but come to an end. That didn't distress me. I wasn't an insomniac. I didn't want to sleep, and I seemed to do fine on the little I got. The nights started getting stranger and stranger. I would sit up at the computer sometimes and work on the books for the practice. I still worried about the practice, but it was doing better all the time. Other times I would walk around the neighborhood or just sit for long periods of time, usually outside. We had set up our exercise bicycle on the porch, and I rode it regularly.

My days were becoming more difficult. I couldn't bring myself to get ready for work. I was becoming less punctual, though I was usually late anyway. I always stopped at Hiebert's on the way to my office to have coffee or breakfast. I lingered there longer and longer guzzling coffee. The antidepressant gave me heartburn, and the coffee really aggravated that, so I carried antacid bottles with me. Once I was at work I could get back into focus and do my job. Your mom figured this out quickly and struggled every morning to get me ready and out the door. Sometimes she had to look around for me. I was rarely in bed.

My thoughts at night were dark and troubled.

Everyone seemed to be out to do me harm, and I could not fully free myself from the anxiety that persisted through the medications Dr. White gave me. I first heard my name called from the dark while I was riding the exercise bike in the middle of the night. It was just my name, but the voice was malevolent. The night was pitch-black. I couldn't see anyone, but I felt as though the source of the voice was within my arm's reach, which was even creepier. The voice didn't tell me anything; it just repeated my name. I got off the bike and went inside for a while. The voice stopped for the time being.

The next night I was just sitting outside wrapped in a comforter when the voice started again. I had a flashlight this time, but that didn't help. I'd look around, but as soon as it was dark the voice would start again. I tried to get used to it. You can't get used to something like that.

One particularly bad night I was sitting outside your room on the front lawn in my chair, wrapped in a comforter. I was there for hours, I guess; I can't recall with certainty. I was detached from time a lot then and frequently dissociated. As the sun came up I became aware of something light-colored in the yard next to me. Eventually it was obvious that it was our pet rabbit, Buck Bunny. He was dead, cold, and as stiff as if he had been stuffed. I don't know why he was dead or what he was doing there in the front yard. The sprinklers must have run earlier, because he was sopping wet. I cried. I wept for that rabbit. That was how your mom found me. She was as puzzled as I was but got me back on my feet and in the shower. I cried and cried for that rabbit. I was so confused. I worried that I had killed the rabbit and didn't even remember it. I never saw the rabbit again.

I had hit a tipping point with my psychiatrist. Dr. White put me on an antipsychotic drug used in schizophrenia. Combined with my other two medications, it made me dizzy. My mouth felt like it was stuffed with cotton and I was a little unsteady on my feet. I felt heavy and dull. It was a strong medication. The voices didn't entirely stop at first.

The crazy stuff continued through what I think was the winter of 1989 and spring of 1990. I was in a sort of race with the medications. I felt as though I was getting worse faster than the medicines could help me. But the antipsychotic became more effective over time. I took more antidepressants. Dr. White and I talked once or twice a week. I worked. Amazingly, I seemed to work well. It was like I had this intense focus on patients that I couldn't muster at other times. When I wasn't working I was often obsessing about how I could get out of my practice now that it was growing so well. I was sure the stress of solo practice was making me crazy. It was my same old error: blaming my mental illness on the circumstances of my life rather than the other way around.

Your mom thought some time off would help. The practice was doing well enough to support a vacation, but I didn't want to leave. Your mother bought a package vacation to San Diego for all of us, and we flew off on our first trip in years. We did Sea World and the zoo and even ventured onto the beaches. I spent the time I didn't sleep at an all-night restaurant up the street from our hotel. I started keeping a journal. I didn't think I could enjoy anything anymore, and your mom proved me wrong. I did feel better that week despite my frightful anxiety. No voices called to me at the restaurant. They were waiting for me at home.

Your loving father,
Dad

Meltdown In
The City By The Bay

Dear Matt,

Once I started traveling more I had a bad experience traveling alone. My favorite place to visit was San Francisco. Up until that time I usually traveled with your mother or one of you. I hadn't gone anywhere very distant alone in years. We hadn't learned yet that I tended to pile up bipolar symptoms (particularly manic ones) in the spring. I felt I was holding it together pretty well on the medications Dr. White had prescribed. The darkness of the previous year seemed to have lightened up, and I felt up to attending the American Back Society meeting. After this trip I didn't travel alone again for a long time.

The trouble started from the day I flew off with anxiety that was almost impairing. It never left. I was staying in the Chinatown Holiday Inn, just walking distance to the meetings at the Hyatt. I never slept but had no trouble staying awake all day. I was too isolated and didn't have my usual routine of caring for patients. I was drinking coffee in my normal heavy manner and having terrible heartburn from the antidepressant. I was eating nearly equal quantities of antacids. I sat in my room for hours at a time just flipping channels as the evenings ran into night and then morning. I'd clean up and wander down the hill past the Transamerica building into the meetings.

One evening I decided that I had to do something different. I walked over to California Street and took the cable car up to Powell and walked to a movie theater on Van Ness. The theater was done in a gaudy plush red velvet motif and looked more like a bordello. I watched *The Hunt for Red October*. Sometime during the film I felt I was losing track of time and had trouble concentrating. It was dark when I came out.

I was at a complete loss for what to do. I couldn't make a simple decision. Go to the hotel? Eat something? Had I eaten dinner? I felt like I had been in the theater for a day. I climbed back onto the cable car. I rode them up and down the streets: California, Powell, Mason, and Hyde. They stop running at midnight, so that was when I first knew for certain what time it was. I was in the financial district when that happened. I just walked around the buildings and by that big funny sculpture on California Street. I could have walked up to Market Street and found some nightlife, but I wasn't thinking clearly and was still struggling to make a simple decision. I didn't want to be alone, but I was afraid to be around another person. I was terrified that I had finally totally lost it. I had that terrible feeling of overwhelming emotional chaos. I was certain I would be picked up by the police and locked in a hospital. Your mom would get a shocking phone call and would have to come get me. I wasn't supposed to fly home for a few days. How could I wait? What could I do? My anxiety had left with the cable cars, leaving pure fear in its place. I was terrified of going to pieces in San Francisco.

Sometime in the early hours of the morning I found myself back in my hotel room. I called your mother in a panic. I was falling apart and thought she could help. She did the best she could to reassure me and try to calm me down. She reminded me that this was nothing I hadn't been through before—it was just happening in a strange city a long way from home. We agreed that I would look into flying home later that day, and that notion was enough to hold my thoughts together. I called her a second time. I thought about calling Dr. White. I was insane and I knew it. I was certain I belonged in a hospital. I was nearly delusional.

I sat on the edge of the bed and looked out the window until the sun was shining on Coit Tower. I felt bolstered. I showered and headed for the Hyatt, stopping at the Cinnabon for my first meal in almost a day. I attended the first few lectures and ate some more at the break. Then I went to the travel agency next-door to the Hyatt and exchanged my ticket for a flight home that afternoon. I was certain the woman helping me could sense my panic. Any penalty for the ticket change was too little to bother with. In no time I was in a shuttle heading for the airport hours before my flight.

You'd think that just getting home would be all I needed to calm down, but it wasn't. I was really worked up and digging around the medicine cabinet for some of my old anti-anxiety drugs to take to put the skids on my emotions. Still, I was greatly reassured just being around your mother again. She was understandably worried. I called Dr. White and saw him first thing the next morning. He had a lot to say about my trip and was concerned about my deterioration. But he didn't think I was becoming a basket case. He thought the change in circumstances coupled with bad timing had set me off. I wasn't ready to be flying off alone yet. He really thought I'd settle down quickly. He was right.

Travel eventually ceased to be a problem. I usually traveled with someone and did just fine for the next several years. You kids frequently accompanied me. I travel alone now and don't have any problems. I enjoy San Francisco again. I did have another mild panic attack in San Francisco years later. Your little brother, Ryan, was with me. It was just before the war in Iraq, and he announced that he wanted to join the military. I had palpitations all night.

Your loving father,
Dad

Me on another trip to San Francisco

Dr. White Disappears

Dear Matt,

Much of the time things were just flipping crazy for me from the time you were seven until you were ten. I was just not around much mentally during that time. My psychotherapy was delving further into my early life. I was an absent father and only marginally involved in you and your activities. The same was true of the rest of the family. Work was everything to me. Dr. White worked with my drugs but was stymied at times by my occasional psychotic symptoms. We talked all the time. I was very talkative, and as I've said, we got further and further into my past.

I don't know how much my past played into my illness, but it was awfully interesting to talk about. An old event that had always had emotional significance to me came up. We talked about the time my mother poured nearly a gallon of boiling water on me while I was playing on the floor in the kitchen. She was boiling it to make a big pot of coffee, I think, and turned and accidentally poured it all over me. I remember turning into one gigantic painful blister. The doctor drove down from the little town up the valley to see me. He wrapped me up in goop and gauze, and everyone stood around and stared at me. I was in pain. I had always assumed I was five or six when this occurred, but Dr. White thought I was probably younger. With one thing and another coming up in therapy I thought it was a good idea to ask my parents about some of my recollections, this one in particular. Do you know what they remembered? My mother thought that just my foot was burned. My dad didn't remember a thing. I was convinced I had made the whole thing up until I asked my brothers about it. My older brother Chuck recalled the incident vividly. He said he hid in the closet the whole day after he saw my burns.

I doubt that event made me a bipolar adult. I don't know that it had much to do with being an adult in any way. However, it does make me wonder what important events I put you kids through that I don't even recall. I hope you'll tell me about them someday.

The years I saw Dr. White were just particularly difficult ones. My disease had just gotten worse. I was not sleeping and was hearing voices. I was paranoid. At the practice, though, I was very busy. The office was booming, and I worked for hours and hours without much of a break. The ambulance service had made it to paramedic level, and I was always out on the streets with them. I was speaking in different states on the subject of emergency medical services. I had a vast photo collection from various emergency scenes. I helped start a paramedic training program and began to teach at the university. My bipolar mania was allowing me to be wildly active and productive.

Dr. White decided to leave town after I'd enjoyed three years of therapy. I was distressed to imagine life without him. I didn't know how I could get through a week without seeing him. I had never been through the process of changing psychiatrists. It was a daunting thought, and I wasn't just distressed; I was really feeling devastated and panic-stricken. Dr. White felt we had accomplished enough—that I would be okay. I quickly realized that I didn't agree with him.

After our last visit I called him up and told him I'd pay him one hundred dollars to meet me once more at Hiebert's for a final session. He readily agreed, and we had our last meeting over coffee and what were advertised as famous steak fingers with chile. It was then that Dr. White agreed to refer me to a new psychiatrist. He recommended a Dr. B. who practiced locally. I never saw Dr. White again. I saw Dr. B. in August 1990, and my life would never be the same again.

Your loving father,
Dad

Dr. B. Part One

Dear Matt,

I recently told Dr. B. this story. I told him that the prospect of calling a new psychiatrist in 1990 was overwhelming. I had never called a psychiatrist who was a stranger. I just ran into Dr. White in the hallway, and I already knew him. I was in a crisis then. Now I was in less of a crisis but no less certain I still needed professional help. I would eventually run out of medications, and even though they only seemed partially helpful, I felt like they were some kind of tether to sanity. I knew by then that whatever was the matter was coming from within me. This was probably the most important thing to come out of my time with Dr. White. I still didn't have it all right, but I was getting there.

I was so uneasy that I had my trusted secretary call to make my first appointment with Dr. B. Anyone who has walked into a therapist's office or called a psychiatrist knows what I'm talking about. I didn't want to expose myself in that way. I took that whole day off and sat at Hiebert's, drinking coffee until it was time to go. That morning I dressed up as if I was attending some kind of special meeting, and I took my briefcase in with me. I wanted anyone who might see me to think I was just there on business and not a patient. I felt like I was nineteen years old walking to John Guzman's waiting room again. I was thirty-six. The clinic was in a small business office complex on a busy street. A strip joint was across the road. The complex had seen better days. It was hot as hell outside. There was nothing fancy about the waiting room compared to Dr. White's very nice office. But it was clean, and I was thankfully alone. They had *The New Yorker* magazines.

I signed in. The staff was very friendly and casual. Some agency somewhere must train persons who work in psychiatry offices to be this way. They were just like the pretty woman in John Guzman's office. My anxiety, which was stratospheric, came down a notch. I didn't wait long before Dr. B. came to the door and asked for me.

He was casually dressed, wore glasses, and had a warm, inviting voice. My first impression was that he was not much older than me but seemed years more mature. I picked up my briefcase and followed him to his simple office. He shook my hand warmly. This was clearly a low-budget outpatient clinic and not an affluent private practice. We sat in a couple of comfortable low-backed chairs on the far side of his desk that did not quite face each other. We exchanged greetings and talked a moment about Dr. White, who Dr. B. knew mostly by reputation. We quickly got down to business.

Business that day was me talking like I only had an hour of life left. I felt like I needed to say everything with the minutes ticking by. My speech was bottlenecked at my mouth. I wanted to sound sane, yet I suddenly wanted this feared stranger to be able to solve all my problems in one visit. The hour was gone almost as fast as it had begun, and it didn't seem like Dr. B. had even twitched a facial muscle. He closed my chart. My heart was racing, and I felt like I had just finished running. I kept right on talking.

"I think you have bipolar disorder," he said. "In fact, I'm certain of it. I would like to start you on lithium before you come back next." That was what he said. I had no idea what it meant.

"When did you want me to come back?" I don't really know what the hell I said. I was so flustered by what Dr. B. had said that I didn't know what else to say.

"Can you come back later this week?" he asked.

I was struck at how I was simultaneously frightened yet relieved that he wanted me back in just a few days. I agreed to come back.

"Are you willing to take the lithium?" he asked. He started to write the prescription.

"Do you really think I need it? I'm already on a few drugs." I was horrified at the thought of taking a drug that I knew nothing about, yet

I was anxious to grasp its benefit as soon as I could.

"This will help you, and you may not need all of those medications once you get stable on lithium. I'll give you the prescription, and you can decide if you want to start it." He handed me the small slip of paper.

My hands were shaking. This was an ancient doctor trick. Once you have that prescription in your hand it is very difficult not to fill it and try it. He knew I'd take the bait. So did I.

That was how our first visit ended. I didn't ask any questions. What the hell was bipolar disorder, and how did he know I had it? Why hadn't Dr. White mentioned it? What was lithium, and what was it going to do to me? I wandered out like an idiot, full of more questions than I had going in. And yet I felt a huge relief. I wanted very much to trust this man and what he recommended, and I was willing to follow through despite my many questions.

Instead of querying him I questioned everyone else: a pharmacist, an internist, and a psychologist. In fact, I went so far as to have the psychologist repeat a personality test on me and see if he thought there was any sign of bipolar disorder. The personality test, a newer version of the Minnesota Multiphasic Personality Inventory that I had taken in college, was a lousy test for problems like bipolar disorder, and he couldn't say one way or another. He did comment on the level of anxiety the results showed.

By the time I saw Dr. B. again, I had just started taking the lithium. I was hoping for some instant result but hadn't noticed anything. Once again he sat without saying a word while I blabbed away. He seemed very interested, just awfully quiet. Dr. White had always asked lots of questions. This guy didn't utter a peep. He increased the lithium dose. Acting like a physician-patient, I had already increased my dose, looking for a quicker effect. This was how our subsequent visit went as well. I didn't know it, but big changes were just around the corner.

Your loving father,
Dad

Lithium

Dear Matt,

Lithium hit me like a brick one afternoon. I was working in my office and running around frantically as normal. I started to feel uncomfortable. I could tell once again that I was feeling drugged. Over the next couple of hours things got very strange. I had the strong sensation of slowing down. I really noticed it in my speech. It felt like my words had become heavy and slow on their way from my brain to my mouth. I couldn't speak quickly, but I still felt a pressure to speak. I could just hardly get words out. Less distinctly, it felt like I was moving more slowly down the hall. Everything I did took noticeable time to do it. Perhaps the next thing I noticed was how much faster my staff seemed to be moving and talking. It was like watching a film that was steadily running faster and faster. Was I moving slower or were they moving faster? I couldn't tell.

Time wasn't going any faster or slower. The patients were backed up in the normal fashion, and the day was long. By the end of the day I was bewildered but in a strange way encouraged that something was happening. I just didn't know what it was and if it was what I wanted.

I don't remember much about the evening. It seemed like you kids were going a thousand miles per hour, and your mom seemed unusually talkative. I just slouched around doing whatever it was that I did. I had never had this experience before, and it was definitely drug-induced. I entertained calling Dr. B. and asking him about what was happening.

That seemed silly. This was probably part of his plan. To the complete shock of your mom, I just went to bed claiming I didn't feel good. I don't know whether I slept, and I think I was up and about later on. I mostly sat and experienced my brain hitting the brakes.

The next day was more of the same, though I seemed to have stabilized at a slower rate of change. I had longer periods between mood swings. Everything didn't seem like it was happening so fast around me. I was less anxious. It seemed like it was taking me forever to do anything, but watching the clock told me I was moving at about my usual pace. It was another strange day. I went to bed early again that night and got up and sat and thought about what was happening to me. I had never had the sense that I was going fast in my mind, but now I had the strong experience of feeling it slow down. I was watching everyone speeding up relative to me. They had never seemed slow. I did notice that I didn't seem to talk as much. Much like my depression in high school, this whole business of slowing down seemed to me to be obvious to the rest of the world. It was not. But one very unlikely person did notice and actually comment to me.

Two attorneys interviewed me one afternoon. I was the treating physician in a workers' compensation suit, and they held a deposition in my office. A familiar court reporter was transcribing the proceeding. I did depositions often. A typical interview like this took hours, largely because of my long-winded responses to questions. The interviews were important, and I usually had a lot of strong opinions that I thought needed to be voiced. As we were packing up at the end of this particular interview, the court reporter leaned over to me. He said that we had just had the shortest deposition he could remember. He had found it interesting that my answers were shorter and that I often answered with a simple yes or no.

"I don't remember you just saying yes or no much before. My fingers aren't even tired from typing."

I didn't give an explanation. No one else seemed to have noticed. I hadn't really even noticed the difference until the court reporter said something.

Conciseness, previously lacking in my medical reports, letters, and legal interviews became more apparent. I'm not sure I was actually concise, but I was much less wordy, and I seemed to convey more with fewer words. I was learning that one feature of bipolar disorder is a strong drive to speak. Speech becomes pressured and fluid. The need to speak was one of those queer symptoms I had no idea I had until it went away along with my forced fast pace. None of this was a surprise to Dr. B.

Your loving father,
Dad

Dr. B. Laughs

Dear Matt,

The next time I saw Dr. B., I had been feeling the effects of lithium for most of the week. I felt like Superman eating kryptonite in my breakfast cereal as I watched my speed, confidence, and energy vanish with the lithium therapy. Dr. B. seemed intensely curious about the changes and what I thought about them. I was ambivalent. He asked a lot of questions. Dr. B. seemed like a different person. There were actual pauses in the conversation. He seemed to think between questions. I wasn't always talking, though I had plenty to say.

He finally asked me, "What did you think about me the first time you came here?"

"I couldn't believe you were a real psychiatrist. You didn't say a thing. I did all the talking. You sat like a damn bump on a log," I said. I think I used stronger expletives.

"What do you think now?"

"I think you've improved a lot. At least you're asking questions and paying attention. This is a lot better," I said. I meant it.

Dr. B. adjusted his glasses. He always did that when he was about to say something important. Dr. B. laughed. Psychiatrists rarely laugh.

"I wish I had videotaped our first visit," he said. "You were so manic it would have been a great tape for the medical students to have seen. You are much improved today. The lithium is working well."

I didn't know what to make of this. I was taking a drug that was

93

fixing a problem that I hadn't known I had. The speeding in my mind wasn't driving me mad—it was the anxiety and all that went with it. But then I hadn't been aware of the speed of my mind. As far as I could tell it felt like the rest of the world was changing. What I really wanted to be rid of was the intense anxiety and fear. I wouldn't have minded dropping the depressed mood too. I could live with the speed and the sleeplessness. Lithium was destined to correct a multitude of sins, some of which I didn't even know needed correcting. I was still fairly ignorant about bipolar disorder.

I think Dr. B. at first assumed that I knew more than I did or that I would be more up to speed, so to speak, by this time. I was embarrassed to ask questions, even though I was still so much in the dark. I was so ignorant that I didn't ask when to quit increasing the dose of lithium. Within a week I was toxic from it and stumbling around like a drunk. My blood level was way over the therapeutic limit, and Dr. B. cut me back to the dose I would take for years.

My anxiety began to improve significantly. I began to sleep more at night and noticed that I was tired at the end of the day, usually long before my day ended. Still I was as busy as ever with the practice and the ambulance and my new position teaching at the community college. I still sat at Hiebert's in the mornings drinking coffee or eating steak fingers and chile. I still dreaded work, but my focus on patient care was better than ever.

Dr. B. seemed like a genuinely kind and smart guy. He seemed very concerned about my well-being and slowly revealed more about bipolar disorder to me. I think he recognized my ignorance and reluctance to look stupid by asking even basic questions. After it was clear I was willing to continue to take lithium, Dr. B. said it would take a year to adjust to it. A year. I thought he was nuts. He was right.

Your loving father,
Dad

You at age 10 in your fedora in San Diego, 1990

You Buy An Acura

Dear Matt,

Early in my relationship with Dr. B. he began to ask about the "Five S's." He inquired about speed, speech, sex, sleep, and spending. Those were the five parameters of bipolar disorder that were usually disordered. When he asked about speed, he asked how overcommitted I was and how many things I tried to cram into a single day and night. My nights were nearly as busy as my days at times. The first time he asked, I had seven paying positions including my practice. I had a family. I was already starting to have trouble keeping up with my manic life as the lithium settled in. Speed included grandiose thinking or planning and elevated self-esteem (which I enjoyed as an exceptional and comfortable confidence) and could even include delusional thinking. One of Dr. B.'s tests for speed was assigning me novels to read to test my ability to sit still and concentrate.

He always asked about my speech, but that was pretty obvious at our visits. I didn't talk anymore like I had a chamber of magma pushing the words out. We could actually converse by then, though I was still very talkative in my work situations and with patients. He asked about sex. I was hypersexual. I wanted and frequently demanded sex from your exhausted mother daily. I was frustrated by her reluctance to meet my demands. He talked to me a lot about this. He was worried about our marriage and surprised that we were still together. He hadn't met your mom yet.

Sleep was a key marker to him. The more I slept the better. I was sleeping more even early in my lithium therapy. Overall I was sleeping more consistently if not a great deal more when I added all the hours up. Finally, Dr. B. always wanted to know if I was spending money excessively. That was hard to gauge. I always spent excessively now that I had money to spend. He asked me specifically one afternoon, "Are you planning any large purchases?"

"No," I said. I was lying to him. This was not the last time I lied to Dr. B.

What I didn't tell him was that I had been cruising the Acura dealer's lot for weeks, counting the cars and learning what the stock was. A massive shift in the local military base had stifled car sales significantly. The first Gulf War was gearing up. The cars may have been moving around the lot, but they weren't selling. One afternoon you and I went down to the dealer and I showed them the Acura Legend I wished to buy. I made them a ridiculous offer and told them I would pay cash. I tossed my checkbook on the salesman's desk. He blubbered like car salesmen blubber when faced with a problem. I was offering a cash deal to a dealer who hadn't moved a car in nearly a month. But the price had to be painful to him. He scurried off to the sales manager.

Of course they would not accept the deal. I knew better. I was still feeling grand and powerful. The lithium hadn't ruined that yet. I knew they would sell me the car for my price. Back and forth we went until we had the sales manager in the office and all the other salespersons standing around the showroom watching. It was starting to get late. Indecision was written in capital letters on their faces.

Finally you piped up and said, "We better get home, or mom will be mad at us."

"You're right," I said. I reached for my checkbook.

"Sold!" the salesman shouted. He slapped his hand on my checkbook. I wrote the check, and we drove home and told your mom. I don't even remember her reaction other than asking if we had the money to do that. I reassured her. I didn't really know if the practice could handle it, but I wasn't worried. I was still manic enough to think money was always sufficient. It was weeks before

I had to fess up to the purchase to Dr. B. I told him it was entirely your fault.

Your loving father,
Dad

A Mixed-Up Disorder

Dear Matt,

Lithium changed me considerably in the fall of 1990. I clearly slowed down, and aside from the Acura I think I spent less. My sleep improved. I had less anxiety that first year, though I was never anxiety-free. I noticed that my confidence was finally shaken. I had looked forward to sparring with attorneys in my frequent depositions, but now I feared them. My practice by that time was primarily workers' compensation patients, and most of them were litigating their cases. I was deposed in almost all those cases.

What was perhaps most prominent those first months was the degree to which I felt overwhelmed by my many professional commitments. The biggest commitment was my practice. It had grown into a highly demanding and very busy operation, and I was working through weekends keeping up with it. I began to feel that I wouldn't be able to maintain it if the changes I was experiencing with lithium persisted.

My response to lithium had one noticeable inconsistency. While my manic symptoms appeared to fade, my sad mood became increasingly apparent. My moods were more depressed than manic. I thought I was primarily manic and should no longer feel depressed. Lithium doesn't treat depression, and so its effect appeared to allow that depression to become more noticeable. Both Dr. White and Dr. B. were aware of my depressive moods. I had been taking antidepressants for at least three years. I thought that depression and mania were cycles that replaced one another in bipolar disorder. I had not heard of a person with both symptoms occurring simultaneously. Even then I had only a rudimentary understanding of my disorder and my medications.

I should not have been surprised when Dr. B. suggested an explanation for my complaints of feeling unhappy. He had felt early in my therapy that what I took as depression was really just a normal mood that had been accustomed to mania. That made sense to me; however, I had always felt a little depressed under all my other symptoms. Dr. B. ultimately concluded that I was suffering from a "mixed" form of bipolar disorder. I was manic and depressed simultaneously. He divided my disorder into three sets of symptoms: feeling, thinking, and acting. My feeling or mood was chronically depressed, while my thinking and my behavior were decidedly manic. I didn't have the normal cycle of depression and mania that is more common in bipolar disorder. I had it all at once.

There was more to come. Worse was the news that the treatment for mixed disorders was more complicated and less effective than that of the normal cycling bipolar patient. The reason was obvious, though it wasn't obvious to me. Treating depression with antidepressants tended to aggravate the manic issues, and suppressing the mania tended to reinforce the depression. This was getting better all the time. The topper to it all was that there was usually little cycling involved in mixed bipolar disorder. My symptoms were likely to remain fairly consistent day to day. In my case it has turned out there is never an abatement of my symptoms but rather some seasonal cycling. Otherwise I'm just the way Dr. B. described me.

I had known something was odd with me all along, really. I would never have put all the pieces together the way Dr. B. did. Over the years he has treated me he has been forced to try an extensive list of drug combinations to try to find one to treat both sides of my bipolar disorder concurrently. Drug combinations are the normal course of treatment. I've experienced many trials and errors. It has proven to be more of a mixed-up disorder.

Your loving father,
Dad

Dumping The Practice

Dear Matt,

At first Dr. B. kept me on the medications Dr. White had started and added the lithium. I was doing the best I had done but felt fatigued by the lithium. I was probably really getting down to my normal energy level, but it sure felt like fatigue to me. Dr. B. emphasized that I would have trouble knowing what was normal after so many years of bipolar mania. He was right; I couldn't tell. After several months I came to the point when I decided my medicated state would make the practice unmanageable. I was working alone and had a bustling pace. The days of staring at empty rooms were a distant memory. I did a lot of consulting, seeing other physicians' patients for chronic problems. I did chronic pain work, and a fair amount of that involved chronic spine pain. This was a challenging and at times demanding group of patients. They were frustrated and tired of their symptoms, and even good medical care often offered them little relief.

An initial visit with me was usually at least an hour and often generated a dozen pages of report. I was good at what I did, even during my worst days. But I was now very unsatisfied with myself and with the practice. Despite the success it was more than I felt I could continue to do. The only way out was to sell the practice. I was still carrying too much debt to just quit. By 1991 I began to let the word out that I was looking to leave.

I had no idea what I would do next. I couldn't bring myself to think about returning to the emergency room, though that was the most likely scenario. It would be reasonable temporarily, but I wasn't sure I could keep up that pace either. I was feeling that slow and tired. Parties were interested in the practice now that it was grossing thousands of dollars a month. At first nothing worked out, despite many meetings and even a trip to a Dallas firm. Selling a medical practice is a touchy thing, because part of what you are selling is your own skills and personality. I was the primary cause of the practice's success, and I would be leaving my successor with no certainty that patients would continue to come to see him or her.

In the spring an out-of-town physician with appropriate experience started making inquiries about the practice. He eventually asked about joining me. I wasn't particularly interested in staying and taking on a partner. One day I received a call from a multi-physician clinic offering a position. It paid 20 percent of what I was netting in my practice, but it offered many benefits, including time off and health insurance. I called the other physician about buying the practice. He readily agreed. By August I was a physician in the new clinic and had sold the practice at an unexpected profit. You cannot imagine my relief. As much as I wanted to cut back, at first I increased my outside commitments to draw in extra income.

The biggest benefit of the change was with you guys. Between the effect of my medications and the shorter hours I worked, I was free to attend soccer and basketball games and concerts. I could take time off, and I was able to take advantage of the effect of the medications to start to become more of a father and husband, something I had sorely neglected over the previous years. I doubt the change was something you would have noticed at the time, but maybe you did. You were eleven by then.

In the new clinic I was working mostly eight to five, with light evening and on-call weekend time. I liked the patients and the clinic structure. I was one of several doctors. Thanks to therapy and the change in my job, I was less distracted in the evenings, and I recall being more involved in what was happening at home. Your mom welcomed the changes, and we never looked back to the lucrative practice with any regret about leaving.

Your loving father,
Dad

The Ups And Downs Of Drugs

Dear Matt,

Despite early success with lithium, it wasn't long until my symptoms required an increasingly complicated and sophisticated drug treatment plan. All bipolar patients—and I'm no exception—have been through at least a few drugs in every major medication category. Part of this is the complexity of the disease, and part of it is the steady arrival of new medications useful in bipolar disorder. Only one of the drugs that I take now was even available at the time of my diagnosis. Everything else has become available in the last twenty years. I bet I can remember what I've taken. The list is long and includes alprazolam, lorazepam, clonazepam, diazepam, imipramine, fluoxetine, venlafaxine, bupropion, thioridazine, quetiapine, ziprasidone, aripiprazole, olanzapine, valproic acid, lamotrigine, lithium, zolpidem, and temazepam. Out of that list I now take seven medications daily.

As my symptoms advanced I changed medications for two reasons: effectiveness and side effects. I experienced the old problem of finding drugs that worked that I could tolerate. The most frustrating medications were the ones that were effective but had unacceptable side effects. A great example of a drug that worked but was intolerable was valproic acid. It is commonly used for seizures and epilepsy but really works well in bipolar mania. I took it for three years to supplement lithium. During the first six months the drug seemed very promising, though I had the disturbing effect of hair loss severe enough to produce thin patches on my scalp. About the time I was ready to stop the medication my hair started to fill back in. Like a chemotherapy patient my hair grew back in tight curls compared to my usual straight locks. The rest of the time I took the medication I looked like I was having perms done. The girl who cut my hair actually asked if anyone could take the drug because of the great curling effect it had.

However effective valproic acid proved to be, the main problem with it was weight gain. I put on over thirty pounds while I was on it. It took two years off of the drug to lose that weight. Weight gain was also a problem with olanzapine, one of the most effective drugs I ever took. Once when I was in a manic crisis it was olanzapine that pulled me out. I just couldn't take it for long because the weight gain was rapid and significant. We kept it as a fallback drug for emergencies.

In some cases increases in doses caused trouble. Your mom and I laugh now about one of our sexual encounters when I was moved to a high dose of fluoxetine. The medication was known to cause delay in ejaculation. Without going into embarrassing detail, we had a failed attempt at sex during a romantic getaway in San Diego. We ultimately ended up on the floor, complete failures, exhausted by our prolonged attempt to complete the act. The problem proved chronic. I didn't think it was funny at the time, but in retrospect we must have looked comical. Dr. B. lowered the dose.

My form of bipolar illness was stubbornly resistant to medications in some ways. One medication would work for a set of symptoms but aggravate another set. Fighting the depression and anxiety were always problematic. Dr. B. is an expert in the pharmacology of bipolar disorder. Still, I've been a frustration for him at times, as he has worked through the almost infinite combinations of medications reported to work in mixed bipolar disorder. I think the last several years of stability that I've enjoyed are sufficient testament to his success in finding a tolerable and effective regimen for me.

The medicines aren't perfect. The antipsychotic drug I take now causes mild weight gain and fatigue. My anti-anxiety medications seem to lose their punch when I have seasonal flares of anxiety. No antidepressant has kept depression from always nipping at my heels.

One of the queerest side effects I recall involved my tremendous coffee habit. Valproic acid, which permed my hair and expanded my gut, made me lose my taste for coffee within a week. Coffee actually began to taste terrible. I just stopped drinking coffee and suffered the predictable headache for the following week. It would be weeks and a new distressing syndrome would arise before I learned that the coffee had been causing more good than harm.

Your loving father,
Dad

Pissing On The Interstate

Dear Matt,

When I stopped drinking coffee because of the new medication, I was still busy chasing my paramedics and their ambulances around the county. It was the early 1990s. I was having dinner alone one evening when a call came through on my pager. A police officer had hit a UPS truck on the interstate. Any accident involving a police car tended to bring out the entire county emergency system. I was on the street with my lights flashing and siren blaring in seconds.

The accident scene was only a few miles north of our house, and I was the first emergency vehicle to arrive after the state police. I came up the off ramp and arrived at the accident facing north in the southbound lanes. All southbound traffic had been stopped. A stream of fire and rescue trucks was coming up the ramp behind me. The damaged police car was a heap of tangled metal pouring various fluids into the middle of the interstate. The car was so smashed that I assumed the officer was dead. The UPS truck was off the side of the road standing upright, with the two shaken occupants standing beside it. The limited available light rapidly gave way to near daylight as more emergency vehicles arrived and switched on their halogen scene lights. I felt as if I would get sunburned.

To my surprise the officer in the police car was alive and conscious. It was a miracle. The firefighters went to work cutting him out of the wreckage. I frequently took pictures at emergency scenes, and I took a few of the police car. I used them for case reviews with the ambulance crews and for educational lectures. I went down to the UPS truck. It showed almost no sign of damage, and the occupants hadn't seen what hit them. I took a couple more pictures and went back to the paramedics at the police car.

I had to pee.

I didn't just have to pee. Within a minute of the feeling I felt the irresistible urge to urinate and realized that I was going to have to find a suitable spot quickly. By that time the scene was crowded with stopped traffic, onlookers, emergency vehicles, and dozens of high-intensity halogen lights. Finding any privacy appeared to be out of the question. I searched the area quickly, increasingly desperately. My only hope was a huge mesquite bush that cast a dark shadow over by the UPS truck. I dodged down there and took what would under normal circumstances have been a very satisfying piss. No one appeared to notice. I felt like it took ages. I went back to the accident scene. Fifteen minutes later I needed to pee again. And again the urge quickly became irresistible. I made it to the shadow just in time and urinated another tremendous volume.

The officer was still in the wreckage, and I'd met again with the medics when the urge returned twenty minutes later. I thought about heading home but realized I didn't have the time. Turning around, I spotted my little vehicle in front of a wall of fire and rescue trucks with police cars parked everywhere. How was I going to get out even if I had time to? I went back to the shadowy bush and did it again.

I said good-bye to the crew, giving some lame excuse for leaving early, and got in my truck. The only escape route was down the embankment toward the UPS truck and then cross-country to the crowded off ramp. I slowly made my way using four-wheel drive in the sand. I had to stop and pee on the way home. By the time I got home I was getting thirsty and had a couple long guzzles of water. Within an hour I was peeing again. This pattern of peeing and drinking kept me up much of the night with about hour-long intervals between each. It was a long night interrupted by urinating and dreaming of pissing on the interstate in front of all those people.

In the morning I called my internist's office and asked if I could catch him before he started seeing patients. Unlike the people who work for psychiatrists, not everyone who works in a doctor's office is warm or compassionate, even to another physician. Still, I got to see my doctor as he came in that morning. I could barely stay out of the bathroom for the extended visit. He tested my urine. It was the same concentration as water. He questioned me extensively. I didn't mention that I had stopped drinking coffee, which was the one essential element that he needed to understand what was happening to me. The cause of my peeing and intense thirst remained a mystery for the time being, and I left the office.

I began to carry an empty quart milk jug in the car, and I always had something to drink with me. I underwent a nightmarish test of my kidneys' ability to concentrate urine as they normally did overnight; I had to go through an entire night without a sip of anything. I barely made it to the doctor's office. I delivered the urine sample and then nearly drowned at the water fountain. My urine was still the concentration of water.

I had a disease called diabetes insipidus. The cause was undetermined. It wasn't until I saw Dr. B. a few frustrating weeks later that the picture became clearer. He recognized that the lithium I was taking caused the syndrome. He also ferreted out my coffee-drinking abstinence. The high volumes of caffeine I had been ingesting had acted to kick the lithium out of my kidneys like a diuretic or water pill. The result was lithium toxicity to the kidneys as soon as I stopped drinking coffee. The proper name was nephrogenic diabetes insipidus.

The solution proved simple. I started taking a daily diuretic that acted like caffeine, and the lithium toxicity stopped. I quit peeing like a Roman fountain the first day I took the medication. The police officer, who it turned out was an old friend of mine, survived the accident. I never pissed on the interstate or in the milk jug again. Water had never tasted so good.

Your loving father,
Dad

The Summer Of 1994

Dear Matt,

One of the worst problems psychiatrists face with bipolar patients is keeping them on their medicines. Think about it for a minute. If the lack of medicines gives you energy and confidence and no need for sleep, who is going to take pills? Notwithstanding my anxiety, I've always missed some aspects of mania. Thus the opportunity that presented itself in 1994 was too good to pass up. I was *told* to stop all my medications. For months I had been complaining to Dr. B. about fatigue. I was certain I needed more antidepressant therapy. He thought I was experiencing daytime drowsiness and wanted to have me take a sleep study. In spite of his better judgment he went along with my request and increased my antidepressant dose. It didn't help. I agreed to the sleep study. I was told to stop all my medications for the study. I did so two weeks before I went to the sleep lab. I was manic by the time I arrived for the study. I sat with the staff in the control room, talking away until nearly 3:00 AM. They finally forced me to go to bed, where I slept about three hours. Sure enough, I had severe sleep apnea, the kind where I would just stop breathing for close to a minute at a time. I think that so distracted Dr. B. that he didn't make sure I had started back on my medications. I had not. The Five S's came back to life. Let me use spending as my primary example of the bipolar mania that followed.

The first of the many events of the summer of 1994 was a trip to San Francisco that you and I took in May. We had a great trip staying at the posh Le Méridien Hotel. We saw the sights that we liked from our previous trips and spent money with abandon. I was planning on working urgent care for a clinic all summer, and I didn't anticipate money being a problem. I recall distinctly how expensive breakfast was, and I didn't give it a second thought.

Less than two weeks after we returned, the whole family loaded up and headed for your uncle's wedding. The wedding included Old West costumes and a brief ride on a steam engine train up into the mountains. We stayed at a nice lodge. I hadn't started working my summer job yet.

Two weeks later I was cruising the San Diego Harbor enjoying a sailing course with J World. I had a splendid time learning to sail; it had become my latest loony passion. The week on the water couldn't have gone better. Unlike my usual sleepy driving, I sped along to California without a drowsy blink, making a short home movie of my trip for Callie. I had that manic need for little sleep. I felt like a competent sailor by the end of the course. I was now ready to buy a boat.

Life without medication felt good. Through June I worked lots of extra hours at the urgent care clinic and piled up the money, or so I thought. I wasn't keeping very close track of income and expenditures, however. I was manic, and my concept of money was all screwed up. I was sped up again. I wasn't sleeping, and sex was at the top of the interest list.

Our eighteenth anniversary in July was spent at a resort lodge in the mountains on an expensive "romance package." It was romantic and indulgent.

Our family vacation that same month took us through Arizona to California. In three hours I bought a beautiful Catalina 22 sailboat at a brokerage in Phoenix. I didn't just buy it—I had it upgraded for a couple more thousand dollars to include a jib roller furler and a new hatch. The financing was bound to be a problem, since I hadn't arranged it before. For the rest of the trip I faxed forms back and forth to our bank to get the boat loan set up by the time we finished our visit to Los Angeles and San Diego. Disneyland was on that agenda, and I threw money around there like it really was Tomorrowland.

Two days after we returned from California I took Ryan with me to Pittsburgh and a lousy meeting of emergency medical service physicians. We spent over one hundred dollars a day on baseball games and more on great meals. We traveled downstate and visited my father's family. Ryan and I stayed at the ritzy Hyatt Regency Hotel.

While we were returning home your mom left for a rafting trip with her sisters. By this time she was becoming increasingly concerned about my spending and vague reassurances. She had never seen me spend so much money so freely since being medicated. I think she was having visions of Acuras. When your mom inquired I told her with confidence that I was earning more than enough working all the extra hours. But I wasn't sleeping, and there was a twenty-two-feet sailboat parked in the yard awaiting a marina slip. It was soon gobbling up hundreds of dollars per month. I estimated that by the time I sold the boat it had cost us more than two hundred dollars every time we had taken it out for a sail.

Your mom returned from her trip with her sisters just in time for us to leave for Denver, where we stayed at a large Sheraton Hotel for more vacation and a soccer tournament. We dined out with the teams and enjoyed the sights of Denver. Once again the money flowed in one direction: out.

As the summer drew to a close, the boat was in an expensive slip, and I was becoming worried that I might be in some financial trouble as the credit card balances grew. Your mom's suspicions had blossomed, and she called Dr. B. to talk about me. He hadn't seen me for months and probably understood what was going on without more information. He called me in for a visit. I was busted. I hurriedly started back on my medications, knowing he would want blood levels, and mine would be zero. The jig was up. My leash was shortened to monthly visits and closer blood level monitoring.

The worst part, though, came with the credit card bills and the boat loan. My income from the urgent care clinic was generous, over twenty-two thousand dollars in three months of part-time work. My bills for the summer exceeded forty-six thousand dollars as best as I could figure. Now I think that it was probably much more than that. I didn't really want to know then. I don't want to know now.

Your loving father,
Dad

The sailboat in 1995

Spilling The Beans

Dear Matt,

Sooner or later it becomes impossible to keep bipolar illness a secret. The first time I had to reveal my disorder was when I applied for my malpractice insurance. They asked pointedly about any mental illness. My answer generated a letter to Dr. B. for more information. I was never denied the insurance, and no further query came from my response. The next situation was my medical license renewal. Interestingly, for years the medical licensing process had not included any questions about mental illness. That eventually changed. Dr. B. had to write another letter. New Mexico has an impaired physician program, but I was always licensed and never referred to the impaired physician committee.

With time I became more comfortable sharing the fact that I suffered from a mental illness. Almost always the early disclosures were when I was in some kind of crisis and needed help or prayer or someone's intervention. My brief suicidal period is a good example of when the knowledge of my disorder spread considerably. Most persons were willing to maintain my confidentiality.

The next persons I think I began to be open with were my closest friends. It proved to be difficult for them. They were all Christians, and they had to reconcile my madness with my Christianity. That is not always an easy reconciliation, even among friends. They were without exception curious about the disorder and have always wanted to know more. The idea that bipolar disorder is a chemical derangement in the brain was new to them, as it is to most persons. At first I received a fair amount of advice about learning to relax or changing my lifestyle. Soon enough they came to grasp the importance of my medications and my problems with stability. My best friends, John and Bill, have seen me through many ups and downs over the years and have been steadfast. They have become very knowledgeable about bipolar disorder. They are a constant support and source of encouragement.

Over the last few years I have become very open about my disorder with co-workers, friends, and my clinic director. My director has been a great ally and has not been afraid to step in when I was in trouble. I've carefully avoided sharing this information with patients. In my role as a general practitioner I see a fair number of patients with psychiatric issues and disorders, and it has always seemed inappropriate to share my own illness with them. I suppose that could be argued either way, but it seemed to me that this information didn't belong in my doctor-patient relationship. I think if I had been truly impaired it would have been an entirely different matter.

The biggest issue with sharing about having a major mental illness has always been the presuppositions of the hearer. My Christian friends found that it brought up issues of faith as well as morality. These came up as we talked about my disorder. A common question was how responsible a mentally ill person could be for their actions. What if those actions were sinful? Could a person with a warped mind have a true faith? There were lots of questions. It was always most difficult for the persons who cared the most for me to handle the information and new perspective on mental illness. I think we were very slow to share the information with you and your siblings. I think you were all in high school before we told you, and even then it was just a little bit at a time. I'll never forget how shocked you and Ryan was that the summer of 1994 had been a great example of bipolar mania.

One of the strongest features of a mental illness is how isolating it is. Your mom likes to say that you are as sick as your secrets, and this has been a secret to many for decades. Not anymore.

Your loving father,
Dad

My Near Brush With Suicide

Dear Matt,

My disorder took another strange turn after years of treatment. I began to think about killing myself. I don't remember what year it was. By the time I was conscious of suicidal thoughts, I had already stockpiled enough medication to do the lethal job without fail, so I must have been working on the idea for a while. Though I was past the point of openness about my disorder, I kept this a secret from everyone at first. I was not sleeping much those days, and I would get up early to go to the gym. It was always dark when I was up. I started getting up at odd times and would get dressed and sit in the living room. The long hallway down to our bedroom was unlighted. The room past the bedroom was always lit in a dim gray light from a distant streetlight that shone through the thin curtains. I used to stare down the hall to that room, which was a den we called our office. I was certain that room was where I would go when I died. It represented a sort of hell. I don't know if it was just me or the light or the medications, but that room looked viciously evil, and my fate seemed tied to it. I don't know how many nights I stood and stared down that hall. Some mornings I couldn't make myself leave for the gym.

I actually told your mom that I was going to kill myself. I was blunt. I had decided I would leave town and do it in some hotel. I was trying to think of a place that we never went so I wouldn't spoil a favorite destination with a macabre memory. Your mom, being your mom, appeared to take this in stride, though she was shocked and frightened. I grieved with tears but didn't waver from my plans to kill myself with an overdose. I thought I had only days left to live—perhaps a couple of weeks. I can't really remember.

Your mom put me in touch with Dr. B. He thought I should be hospitalized and asked if I was willing to do something like that. Even in my suicidal state of mind there was some appeal to the idea. I was fully medicated, and that course of action appeared to be his only card to play. Your mom didn't want me hospitalized. She was confident that between Dr. B. and herself she could get me through my suicidal intentions. I don't know if she was that certain or deep in denial. She watched me carefully and made sure I went to bed when she did. She often got up in the middle of the night when I did. She made sure I cleaned up and went to work in the clinic every day. At work I was barely functioning, seeing far fewer patients than were expected of me. I finally had to explain my situation to the clinic manager, who proved to be as good a friend as manager. She quieted the complaints about my poor performance and encouraged me every day. Once again someone who didn't have to help me went beyond his or her duties to bail me out. Dr. B. insisted I let the clinic psychiatrist in on what was happening, since he was the most likely person to have to admit me to a hospital. I gladly did these things. I felt I wasn't going to be around long enough to have to worry about the repercussions of my revelations. I think I also felt desperately crazy and fearful of what I was thinking.

I spent a lot of time alone, despite everyone's efforts to keep me busy. I cried frequently. I was grief-stricken at the thought of saying good-bye to your mom and you guys, but I was determined to kill myself. The paradox of desiring suicide and grieving has persuaded me that suicide is a bizarre aberration in thinking and logic that makes no sense from outside the patient. I no longer think I really understand any given suicidal patient's thinking.

I can't remember how long this went on. I think it was just a couple of weeks, but I really have poor recall of a lot of the details. My medications were changed, and the stockpile of pills that I planned to use were found and destroyed. Little by little the desire to kill myself ebbed into thoughts of death and then passed. It was either courageous or stupid of Dr. B. and your mother to try to manage me outside of a hospital. But hospitalizing me would not have been without its stigma and consequences for me as a person and a physician. I'm grateful that everything worked out the way it did, and again I have to thank persons who came to my aid at just the right time. I figured you needed to know about this one.

Your loving father,
Dad

The Garage

Dear Matt,

As the spring of 2001 blossomed I began to speed up. My medications hadn't changed, but I appeared to be changing. Dr. B. had begun to suspect a seasonal acceleration in the spring, but it hadn't been very serious until then. Anxiety arrived. I noticed that I was talking more and felt pressure to speak. I was having trouble keeping to my budget and was not sleeping particularly well. My sex drive was up. There were lots of warning signs in the Five S's, but we weren't used to this spring pattern yet.

Then your mom and I went to Colorado as chaperones for a school trip. As you know, a chaperone's life on these trips is not an easy one. We run herd on students day and night. The nights were particularly challenging since we were usually up until 2:00 or 3:00 AM patrolling the halls and outside the hotel, keeping kids in their rooms and quiet. I felt less need for sleep, and I became more obsessive. We had a gorgeous room with a full view of the snowy Rockies and a massive king-sized bed. But when it was finally time to go to bed, sex was not on my mind. I stayed up reading different newspapers, fixated on Israel barricading Yasser Arafat as if that was the most important thing in my life. I may have slept an hour a night. By the time the trip ended I was experiencing bipolar mania.

When we returned I didn't feel like I should work. I thought I was much too distracted to be good at patient care. I went to my director and explained what I thought was going on. We agreed that I should take leave until I could see Dr. B. in a few days. Those few days away from work turned into a few weeks. I'm very goal oriented when I'm manic. Usually I am best at focusing on practicing medicine. I wasn't this particular time. Rebuilding the garage became my new obsession. I had a brilliant idea to transform it, though we didn't have the money for such a project. I started in one corner and every day built new shelves and specialized spaces for welding equipment and lumber and metal. The ladder and paints and car supplies all got new cabinets or shelves or hangers. Your mom recalls that I would leave the house in the morning and return anytime up to hours later with a new tool and lumber or construction material and then start building more shelves or cabinets. I threw out trash as I went along. I was obsessed with that damn garage.

For the first time I was angry. I don't know where the anger and irritability came from, but I was quick to pop off at your mom. She says that I showed more anger toward her in those couple weeks than I had shown in twenty-five years. Irritability and anger are common features of bipolar mania; I had just never experienced them before. We've added irritability to the Five S's. Not surprisingly, Dr. B. got involved early on and started me on a new antipsychotic drug. Within two weeks I settled down to a manageable state. The drug was amazing. It was also very fattening, as I was later to learn. After I stabilized I tried to return to work. My director insisted on reassurance from Dr. B. that I could return to work, so I had to wait until they finally talked.

We held an open house for my friends to admire the garage that despite my craziness was quite an impressive job. They were impressed. Although the garage job took weeks when it should have taken days, it did end up more functional and organized than it had been, and the changes have been maintained until today. The garage is a good example of how even at my worst I could become hyper-focused on a task. The cost proved substantial and well outside of our budget. The credit card balance climbed once again. But it *is* a great garage.

Your loving father,
Dad

Bipolar Patients I've Known

Dear Matt,

Early in my care Dr. B. asked me if I had ever diagnosed a bipolar patient. Given the years I had been a primary care physician, I was bound to have seen at least a few. They are actually fairly common patients in emergency departments, though less so in clinics.

I said no.

"Don't worry about it now, but you'll get very good at it," he said.

The only bipolar patient I knew about was a regular patient of the emergency department. She would stop her medicines and become manic. Her family, exhausted, would bring her in. She knew the routine and would wander around the department waiting to be admitted to the psychiatric ward. She took requests for songs, and she would sing to the patients. Gregarious didn't even begin to describe her mood. The patients enjoyed her. Our ward clerk's favorite song was "La Paloma Blanca," and the patient always sang that for us. Easy diagnosis.

Subsequent to my diagnosis and treatment, I did begin to recognize the disorder much more often. Sometimes the diagnosis was obvious: the incredibly overdriven and overcommitted young woman with cyclical depressions. Her marriage did not survive her successful therapy. Another obvious person was a young man who spent his nights on his "art," drawing furious scribbles with crayons while bringing transients home to visit. His roommates brought him in. He did not do well with treatment despite the clinic psychiatrist's efforts. Other patients

121

have been subtler. I think one bipolar patient came close to suspecting me of being bipolar from my apparently extensive knowledge of the disorder.

"Are you bipolar?" she asked. "You seem to know an awful lot about it."

I avoided the question.

One patient stands out among all the bipolar patients I've ever recognized. She had red hair, soft features, and a stunning figure. She sat on the exam table uncomfortably and unsuccessfully trying to pull down an overly short skirt to a more modest length. Her parents accompanied her. She was in her early twenties.

Her story started with a tale of a nonstop spending spree. The credit card balances never went away, though her parents paid them regularly while encouraging frugality. She wouldn't tell me how many credit cards she had. No one seemed to know. What was all the spending about? It seemed to be for clothes, partying, friends, and many indeterminate expenses that were apparently never well accounted for.

Her immodest dressing style and flirtatiousness was another issue. She was a party girl and self-described "bar hopper." Did she pick up guys in bars? She wouldn't say. She rarely slept more than a few hours a night and sometimes not even that much. She exhausted her friends but didn't seem to need sleep.

The girl's speech was fast and fluid. There was a pressure behind her words. Her life seemed gay and pleasant. Paradoxically, she described her mood as depressed. She had entertained thoughts of suicide recently. She was pervasively anxious about everything. She spoke freely in the presence of her parents. I found that even more unusual. She had signed a consent form to allow them in the exam room and for us to discuss her medical issues.

It was obvious she was bipolar. What was more, she appeared to be of the unusual "mixed variety," with a depressed mood but manic thinking and behavior. Of course this was the same as my diagnosis. I felt a kinship with this patient that I didn't usually experience. I could have sat down with her, and we would have been able to share many similar experiences. That was not to be. She was a patient, and that type of information about my own condition was entirely inappropriate.

She was not keen on the idea that there was anything wrong

with her or with the idea of starting a medication. Her parents were frantic. We agreed on another visit, and I would work on having her see a psychiatrist. Our next visit was much more of the same speed, spending, speech, lack of sleep, and sex discussion. The Five S's were readily apparent. By then she was scheduled with the psychiatrist. He saw the patient and confirmed my diagnosis. I received the standard consultation letter from him. He insisted that she not see me again. I think he recognized that it was not prudent to have me seeing this young woman, knowing, as he did, about my own disorder. Sadly, I had to agree. Somehow the psychiatrist coaxed her into starting a medication. She didn't like it. I hadn't liked it either when I had taken it.

Still, she kept in touch with an occasional phone call. Then I quit hearing from her entirely. One day a letter from her showed up with a photograph inside. I was afraid to imagine what it showed. It was a picture of twelve credit cards all neatly cut in two.

Your loving father,
Dad

Parkinson's Disease

Dear Matt,

This great misadventure started with stumbling. I couldn't do step aerobics in January of 2003 because I started tripping over the steps. The time came when I had to quit the steps and just do the aerobic moves on the floor. That seemed silly and useless, so I quit aerobics altogether and went back to my old routine at the gym. I was going through a new course of drugs, and I assumed it was just a side effect of the new medications. I developed a small hand tremor about the same time. Over time this worsened and was most pronounced when I was at rest. Again I assumed this was a transient side effect and would get better. Everything got worse.

As the spring progressed, so did my symptoms. The changes developed slowly and were hard to spot at first. One was difficult to articulate: muscle rigidity. My muscles all seemed stiff and moved with more than the usual effort. This was very subtle at first, but as it worsened it affected my fine motor skills, such as handwriting. My writing got smaller and more erratic, and at times I could barely write at all, even sign my name. My anxiety increased, and my appetite dropped. Between being measured for a tuxedo for your wedding and picking it up two months later, I had lost so much weight that it no longer fit and everything had to be changed. I remember how anxious I was trying on the new clothes. All of the male wedding party was there at the store. I could not manipulate the studs to the tux and had to ask for help. I couldn't walk in the shoes with their polished soles without slipping.

You'd think I would have been panic-stricken over these new symptoms. Panic is a physical expression of anxiety. I would commonly have heart palpitations and trouble breathing. It was unusual to have such physical symptoms with plain anxiety. I was more stricken with horrible anxiety from the problems I was having. Dr. B. tried a different medication. It was a change from a similar medicine, so I wasn't surprised when the "side effects" didn't resolve. I was worried about these symptoms, but I just lumped everything together and blamed the new pills.

I don't know how I got through your wedding, Matt. I was too frightened to even drive. I was so nervous about the slippery shoes that your mom and I went out and bought some new ones with normal soles. I was unsteady even in these. Despite all that was happening, your wedding was a great and joyful affair. It was by the grace of God that I was able to participate.

Through the fall, I continued to deteriorate. None of my physicians seemed to understand my symptoms at first, since they were so much like the side effects of the medications I had been taking. Work became increasingly difficult with my anxiety, the peculiar muscle stiffness, and poor handwriting. I shuffled. My face looked old and drawn. I had lost over twenty pounds. The crisis finally came in the oddest way. I was preparing to suture a young man's finger, and while he was with the x-ray technician he said he was uncomfortable with me because I looked "out of it." I did look out of it. I had another doctor do the repair.

The following day I was called to see the medical director. He had been told I had fallen asleep while suturing this patient's finger. I did fall asleep often in those days, but I assured him that I hadn't even done the suture repair. He had actually been concerned about me for a while and had another physician checking my charts for the appropriateness of care. Nothing wrong turned up from that review. The next morning I was put on leave with no specific end point. I was nearly hysterical. I spoke to Dr. B., who recommended that I get my drug levels drawn. I didn't do it.

One November morning early in my leave, one of my best friends, Bill, told me how much I reminded him of his father when he had suffered from Parkinson's disease. Bill could describe every symptom I was having. That was enough for me. I was in my doctor's office, once again, on no notice. Your mom came along, and he looked me over for Parkinson's disease. I had the right symptoms. Even my internist appeared worried through his usual cheerful demeanor. He scheduled me for an MRI of the brain and a neurologist consult and had a slew of blood tests drawn. His suspicion even then was that I was experiencing drug toxicity and not true Parkinson's disease. I didn't believe him.

I didn't sleep that night. Not one moment. I had never experienced unintentional sleeplessness like that. I moved around the house with an insomniac's feelings of helplessness. I barely made it through the MRI in the morning, feeling restless and claustrophobic. I spent the rest of the day feeling cold and old, wrapped in a blanket on the couch. Though I was very tired, I was afraid to try to nap during the day and make it more difficult to fall asleep at night.

That evening my doctor called to tell me that my lithium level was in the lethal range. He was persuaded that was the cause of my symptoms. I couldn't believe it. I was so incredulous I had my level redrawn the next morning and even took my morning lithium dose. The result was even higher than the first level. I was lithium toxic and had been for most of a year. I really had Parkinson's syndrome, a rare complication of lithium toxicity. No one knew if it was reversible with withdrawal of the lithium.

Lithium toxicity takes four months to clear. I was cold and sleepless for weeks. My muscles and balance were slow to return to normal. I was allowed back to work a little at a time. It was a miserable recovery, but my doctor had been correct. The only thing that didn't return to normal was my kidney function. It had been abnormal for a couple of years, and now it worsened. We all assumed that it would recover as well.

By the late spring, over a year after everything started, I was okay. No evidence of Parkinson's disease for me. My kidney function was still abnormal, but Dr. B. insisted I start back on lithium with very careful monitoring. I did, reluctantly. He remained puzzled at how the level of lithium in my blood could have become so high. The level had been monitored dozens of times over the years, and it had always been within the right range. Why it had crept so high remains a mystery.

So I made it back on lithium. My anxiety cooled, and I had one of the more stable years I've experienced until my kidney trouble came back to haunt me the next year. I never looked at the side effects and risks of medications the same after 2003.

Your loving father,
Dad

Me at your wedding in 2003 at the height of my
parkinsonian symptoms

No More Lithium For Me

Dear Matt,

My kidneys refused to improve. I finally asked to see a group of kidney specialists I knew in Albuquerque. The news was not good. I had lithium-induced kidney failure, and it was much more advanced than any of us had realized. The internal structure of the kidneys was badly damaged, and that accounted for my previously mysterious anemia and my new high blood pressure. Both of those problems are caused by kidney failure. I had to stop the lithium and hope for the best. The best was that I would not progress into complete failure and dialysis and transplant. I was fairly well freaked out, but your mom thought the specialist was trying to be upbeat and that without the lithium I would probably not worsen. I had worked in dialysis clinics and dreaded kidney disease.

All of this kidney business left Dr. B. in a lousy position. As far as he knew, the psychiatric medical information available did not show sufficient proof to implicate lithium in kidney failure. To the kidney specialists it was a slam-dunk diagnosis. In addition to that conflict of thinking, he was now forced to find a new drug to replace the one that had been the mainstay of my therapy for over a decade and a half. I wouldn't take lithium again. I didn't envy Dr. B., and I didn't welcome the prospect of going through another whole string of drugs looking for a new version of lithium. Dr. B. wasn't very happy. Neither was I. There weren't a lot of drug choices left. By this time I had been on nearly every drug used to treat bipolar disorder in one combination or another.

We initially blamed my Parkinson's symptoms on the antipsychotic medicines. But I had done well with one of them during the Garage Affair without any weird effects, other than weight gain. By this time these drugs were no longer used just for the worst forms of bipolar disorder and other psychoses. They were being heavily marketed for any form of unstable bipolar disorder that was unresponsive to other medications. I knew the routine. Start on a new medication, and start with a whole new set of side effects. I was already on six medications, four for my bipolar symptoms. Introducing another medication invited new drug interactions.

I was less than enthusiastic, but I had to admit, as I had to admit many times before, that uncontrolled bipolar disorder was destructive for me, and something had to be done to control it. By now I had been seeing Dr. B. for fifteen years. I had the greatest trust in his judgment. I argued that maybe I would not become fully manic again without the lithium. However, I had not done well while off of it the previous spring. I had slipped easily back into sleeplessness, irritability, and anxiety. The Five S's had all returned in one form or another. He persuaded me to start a new antipsychotic.

The most noticeable side effect of the new medication was sedation. Not a little drowsiness—downright sleepiness. I slept at night all right but this was only a side effect, not a natural sleep. I could fall asleep any time of day without effort. I could hardly stay awake. Trying to get to the proper dose, I started taking the medicine at night. The daytime drowsiness persisted. As the summer wore on I wore out despite the clear benefit of the medicine on my symptoms.

The medication made me become flat and indifferent. Nothing much bothered me, but then not much was very pleasurable, either. I made it through a great family vacation with all of you kids in San Diego without any problem, other than trouble engaging in such things as beautiful cool weather, you guys, the beach, and a luxurious seaside hotel. By the end of the summer I asked to change medications.

The only choices left in that limited group of drugs were those I had taken before. I hadn't liked any of them, but I hadn't liked anything during my Parkinson's year. Dr. B. picked the one with the best current recommendations, and I started off on a new adventure. Drowsiness was not a side effect, but it left me feeling tired during the day. It was more fatigue than sleepiness. But there was more: no libido. I experience almost complete indifference to life's ups and downs. It is a strange feeling to not feel much at all. Patients on antipsychotic drugs have always had trouble staying on them, and this is one of the reasons. Life becomes pretty monochromatic. I was no different. However, my symptoms remained mostly under control, and the side effects moderated. Within months my best friends, my director, and your mom all agreed that I was the most level and consistent that I had been in years, if ever. I was still unhappy with the side effects but glad to be so free of other symptoms. My anxiety appeared controlled and my depression just smoldering.

I think Dr. B. knew that some of the decisions he had to make were going to be hard on me. He appreciated my concerns, and over a couple of months we debated trying a lower dose. Finally he cut it in half. No change. I stayed stable but still as flat as an old soda. What about going lower on the dose? Now everyone got nervous, and I was told that maybe we could try it during the winter, when I was typically more depressed and less manic. But the winter came and went with everyone still thrilled with my stable status. My job performance had seemed to improve.

My speech slowed down and pared down. I was lacking any grand schemes. I had much less sex drive. My spending was well within my budget. I was just a little too flat. I wish I could better articulate the feeling of not feeling, but that is about it. I sat through my father's last days in the hospital and finally our decision to take him off life support almost dispassionately.

As usual it was your mother who came to my rescue. She had been aware of the changes in my mood from the medication. She sensed that I was slightly overmedicated. It was her willingness to reduce the dose of the medication further that persuaded Dr. B. to give it a try. That did the trick.

The lights came back on. I could converse again. I could feel again. I was capable of several emotions that seemed to have been absent for months. My sex drive improved. But fundamentally I remained free of most serious bipolar symptoms. We haven't changed a medication

131

since then; it's the longest I've gone without a major drug adjustment. It isn't a perfect combination, but it is the best I've had. In the past, my strong seasonal cycle required us to increase or decrease doses of some medications. This unheard-of quiescence of my disorder has allowed me many hitherto lost abilities, including the capacity to finally write to you.

It is no surprise that Dr. B. responded to your mother's opinion that I could be tried on a lower dose. By now he had developed a great deal of confidence in her observations and suggestions concerning me. He began to refer to her as my "other doctor."

Your loving father,
Dad

Single Mother

Dear Matt,

For years your mom lived as if she were a single mother. It started in 1981 when I first drifted into bipolar mania. By the next year I was actively overworking in emergency rooms around the state. As my symptoms progressed I became more and more of a workaholic. I wasn't a totally absent father. I was usually at my calmest when I was with you guys, often in the evening. I would read to you and play trucks or other games on the floor. When you were older and I was more available in the evenings, I would read whole books to you guys. But far too much of the time I was gone chasing ambulances or locked away with the computer working on business or away on other outside activities.

A couple of incidents might help illustrate some of my absenteeism. One afternoon I finished a deposition early, and I was ready to leave the office at five thirty. This was very early for me. I called your mom and told her I was on my way home. Because it did seem like I had a lot of time on my hands, I stopped by the ambulance station just to check in. I left my cellular phone in the car. Three hours later your mom was frantically trying to find me.

I was busy at the station talking over cases and looking at reports and generally oblivious to the time. Your mom finally dialed 911 and had me paged. That woke me up to the hour, and I was home by nine o'clock to a chilly reception and a very cold dinner. I left early the next morning for a meeting and then went on to the office. I didn't get home until my more usual hour of seven or so. I had just sat down to dinner when my pager announced a shooting in a nearby community. My pager could be switched on to a monitor mode so that I heard every call that went out. I didn't have to do that, and I certainly didn't need to go to every interesting call that came through. But that was how I had it set up. I got up and went to the shooting, returning late to the same dinner sitting where I had left it on the table.

The following morning I had another early meeting, and as I was leaving your mom stopped me at the door.

"Are you having a problem with being married?" she asked. Her tone was acerbic. "Don't you like being at home?"

I denied having any problems with being married or home. I was just very busy with work, and I had to be gone a lot. I gave some lame excuse like that. These incidents were the norm for me at the time, and I had no idea of the root cause of my behaviors. She didn't say anything more. My behavior changed little after that.

Your mom says she rarely ever thought of leaving me. I'm amazed that she never mentioned it or acted on the thought. I don't know if she would have missed me; I was hardly around to start with. I think the times when she really thought about it were later, when my mania triggered anger and irritability toward her. I was at the least mildly verbally abusive. She says it was the toughest before I was diagnosed. But some of the worst episodes came after my diagnosis, when I continued to exhibit the Five S's despite medication and therapy. These were hard because she had come to expect better behavior.

Your mom is a fascinating woman who has the most straightforward approach to life of anyone I've ever known. I want to use the word *simple*, but it suggests a lack of intelligence or subtlety. She lacks neither. But she can see things in the simplest of terms and unlike me does not tend toward cluttering problems and issues with irrelevant muddle. She doesn't think of her early life as hard, but it was certainly challenging. While she was growing up she lived her summers on an isolated ranch and spent her winters in the Midwest. She had a kind but alcoholic father and an angry mother. She was nearly the youngest of five girls. She is an orphan now.

For years my bipolar disorder was as great a mystery to her as it was to me. Even after my diagnosis we both had a great deal to learn.

She views it as a biochemical disease of my brain with psychological symptoms and spiritual implications. She never ceases to pray for me to be compliant with my therapy and improved or healed. She wants me to be happy and successful. She prays for me to be given strength as a husband and father. Your mom sees me in much more positive terms than I see myself and is less critical about most of what I've written about than I am. Still, I think her time living with me has not been easy, and a weaker woman would not have held up. Your mom thinks she is shy and a wimp. She is made of steel.

I've gotten to know her better in the years since my diagnosis than in all the years before. I continue to learn about her. Your mom thinks I have given her a good life; I think it could have been better. She was always there for you kids when I was not. In addition, she always had room for me in her life despite my husbandly shortcomings. I love your mother dearly and admire her greatly. You will meet few women of her caliber in your life.

Your loving father,
Dad

Your pregnant mom with you and Ryan during
my fellowship in 1983

The Shaman

Dear Matt,

Almost thirty years after I last saw a psychologist I returned to see one I'll call the Shaman. A psychologist holds a PhD degree and is not a medical doctor. A psychologist cannot prescribe medications but uses psychotherapy as his or her primary tool. Dr. White and Dr. B. were medical doctors and psychiatrists. I was long overdue for psychotherapy, something I had enjoyed to some degree with Dr. White. I've decided that anyone who thinks they can tackle a major mental illness without the help of both a psychiatrist and a good psychologist is missing out on half of their care. I'm substantially better off for the talk therapy I had with Dr. White and the counseling I've had with the Shaman. Bipolar illness is a many-faceted disorder, as are most serious mental disorders, and this man helped bring order to a lot of chaos. Who doesn't need a psychologist like the Shaman? Dr. B. appreciates the help I get from the Shaman. It takes a burden off of him and lets him do what he is really good at: medication therapy.

One autumn day I was tearful and agitated at work. I was worked up about your brother, Ryan. It had suddenly struck me that he had gone from being my child to being an adult in a very short period of time. He had been in the air force for over a year. We hadn't invaded Iraq yet, but he was heading to Kuwait as part of the prelude to war. I felt a great loss and grief. I was showing some bipolar symptoms of depression that we have come to call the "fall glooms." I was able to get into the Shaman's office right away.

I cried at the Shaman's office. Actually I bawled from the minute I walked in until I left. I lay on the floor for quite a while, and he touched me on the back. I couldn't stop crying. Now that I look back on the visit, I don't even know if I told him what I was crying about. It had to be the single best visit to a psychologist I've ever had. He really was a shaman: wise and caring and deep. Needless to say, we had to pick up the pieces over the next few weeks. I strongly wanted to go to Lackland Air Force Base, where Ryan had done basic training, and walk through the places we had walked through after his graduation. I thought I had ghosts there that I needed to resolve. I felt like I hadn't really been there for him at that important time. I wondered if going back to Lackland and retracing our steps would help me. No one thought it was a good idea. I still think it was.

It took me a long time to accept the fact that Ryan, my boisterous blond-headed scamp, had become an adult. I didn't know an easy way to let go. In addition to seeing the Shaman, I had to have my medications adjusted again, increasing my antidepressant. Shortly after my meltdown Ryan went off to war. I was better at dealing with that whole experience than I would have been without the help of the Shaman.

In no time my bipolar disorder became the focus of my discussions with the Shaman. Psychologists take a different angle on bipolar disorder. They see it much as any other psychological disorder, with origins at least partly in life experiences growing up and coping. The strictly medical model of chemical derangement was my point of view. Over time we both changed our views, and I have come to accept his rather convincing arguments that there are some strong psychological elements to my disorder. He became interested in my medications and their benefits in my treatment. In addition, his intelligent counsel helped address many of the dysfunctional ways in which I had tried to cope with my disorder.

Still, his primary focus has always been on how I feel about things. Digging up new and old feelings sounds like a cliché, but with someone with the wisdom of the Shaman it proved repeatedly productive. He has degrees in divinity, psychology, and counseling. He is a contemplative person who once studied for the priesthood. He ponders questions and speaks in a low and soothing voice. Insight fills his words. I still enjoy seeing him.

Much has happened since I first saw the Shaman. You and your sister have both married, and I have done much better at coming to terms with everyone growing up and leaving home. I can't say I like it. Change does not come easily to a bipolar person. I'm sure that in the future I'll have a lot of changes to come to grips with.

Your loving father,
Dad

Ryan, your mom, and Callie at Ryan's completion of
basic training in 2001

Thoughts About
Psychiatry And Dr. B.

Dear Matt,

There are not enough pages to recount the many years that I have seen Dr. B. We've been through a lot of problems and a lot of therapy. He has always combined a kind of subtle psychotherapy with the medications. I've come to admire and dearly love the man. I credit him with saving my marriage, my relationship with you kids, and my ability to maintain my professional standing. He has saved my life. I still see him monthly after nearly two decades. I've not always been an easy patient to manage. We had some bad times. For me bipolar disorder includes lots of spin-off problems, including obsessive-compulsive disorder and attention deficit disorder. Dr. B. has had his hands full at one time or the other trying to manage all the screwball facets of my illness.

Occasionally I'll have some resident physicians in psychiatry or medical students sit in during our sessions. I don't know what they think of a mentally ill physician. I don't know what I would have thought as a medical student. Your mom is a frequent guest. Dr. B. welcomes her clarity of thinking, recall, and unquestioned veracity. I don't think he always believes that I tell him the whole truth. I don't know that I always know the truth.

There is no describing the relationship you develop with a psychiatrist over years. I remember training in psychiatry, but it seems as though everything I learned was either out-of-date or completely irrelevant to being a psychiatric patient by the time it was my turn. My training was in the inpatient unit of the Bernalillo County Medical Center. In that era only the first generations of antidepressant and antipsychotic drugs were available. I've taken drugs from both of those old groups, and they are not pleasant. I only worked with patients who were no longer functional in the real world and were locked in a psychiatric ward. They were taking side-effect-laden medications, waiting for improvement that seemed awfully long in coming. The patients were the worst example of psychiatry of the time. These patients were not functioning at any level in life outside the facility's doors.

My training had little resemblance to sitting quietly and comfortably with Dr. B (or Dr. White or the Shaman, for that matter) examining my personal status. The psychotherapy I receive is personal and focused. I've been able to stay outside of the inpatient facilities.

I don't really know Dr. B. well. I am certain he is married and has children, but I've never heard too much about them. His daughter is a physician. I don't know what his wife does, and I only know a few things about his personal activities. He went to Italy once. His office is full of awards and gifts that reflect respect and affection. I used to know what he drove, a Mazda 929. In spite of this paucity of knowledge, I would describe him as an open and friendly man. I just pretend I know him well.

Dr. B. will retire someday. I don't know what I'll do when that happens I've seen him for many of the years he has been in practice. I'm certain I'll have to start over with a new doctor or maybe see a couple of new doctors before settling down again with a new psychiatrist. I imagine in my mind that will never happen and I'll be cured before Dr. B. retires. I want medicines to work and not have side effects. I want to please Dr. B. and stay stable. There is nothing left that is too personal to tell him and little that is an embarrassment. Still, the day is coming when all the years together will come to an end and I'll be sitting down with a new face, doubtless younger than mine, and saying, "I have bipolar disorder."

Your loving father,
Dad

Paying For Things

Dear Matt,

Well, someone had to pay for all of this expensive mental health care. Despite having insurance, we've carried the burden of a lot of my care. The cost has come in the form of insurance premiums, deductibles, and co-payments. I think I am fortunate to have insurance, but I'm not sure it has been that much help. Once I had the diagnosis of bipolar disorder I no longer qualified for individual health insurance. That was one of the reasons I took the new position with the clinic: it offered group health insurance that could not turn me down.

Of course, I'm also no longer able to purchase life or disability insurance. Health insurance is not inexpensive, but for us it seemed a necessity. A monthly visit to a psychiatrist or psychologist has a substantial cost, and health insurance appears to mitigate that to some degree. Over the years the degree to which our health insurance paid for mental health therapy has varied considerably. Early in my treatment I would just have to pay up to the deductible and then pay a percentage of the cost of each visit. I appeared to save about half of the cost of my care with insurance. However, when we added in the cost of the insurance it would have been less expensive to just pay for all of my care and medications out of our own pocket. The insurance was an added cost and not a cost saver. Not until later in my therapy did the cost of my mental health care and my medications in particular approach the cost of the monthly insurance premiums.

After several years deductibles went away, and managed care arrived on the insurance scene. Significant changes occurred in how my bipolar disorder was managed. I no longer dealt with the insurance company directly. I had to contact a contractor who handled mental health problems separately. I called a toll-free number and had to request permission to see my psychiatrist or psychologist. I was given authorization for a limited number of visits, and I would have to request additional visits during the year. Payments by the insurance company for my care dropped, and I had to pick up an even bigger share of the cost. Once again, when the costs of the insurance premiums were added in, the insurance was not a cost saver at all.

The time came, however, when the balance began to tip in my favor. Our most recent insurance plan expects me to make a modest co-payment for each visit and pays for the rest of the fee. That alone would not be enough to make up for the cost of the premiums if it wasn't for the fact that they also pay a substantial portion of my medication costs. My recent medication costs have been as high as nine hundred dollars per month. One medication I take costs more per ounce than gold. Now our insurance premiums and my cost of care are nearly equal or weighted in favor of the insurance saving us money.

So what good has the insurance done for us? We've spread our costs out throughout the year in the form of premiums that are a predictable sum every month. When problems have arisen that would be very expensive, such as diagnosing my Parkinson's syndrome, the insurance clearly saved us money. I can have the latest and most expensive therapies without fear of their costs. Persons without insurance don't have those options.

Still, there is no insurance plan that protects you from all your losses with bipolar disorder. I suffered fewer losses than patients who have lost their marriages and families, their jobs or careers, and their battered self-esteem. Still, I had real losses that no insurance was going to protect me from.

Your loving father,
Dad

My Spirituality And
My Medications

Dear Matt,

At the time of my diagnosis I was a zealous and enthusiastic Christian. I was a regular and serious student of the Bible. I taught a popular Bible study at church. The truths of the Bible seemed real, and Jesus felt very personal to me. Where I had started with little more than an emotional need, I had grown greatly to have an emotional and intellectual grasp of Christianity. I was considered a mature man of God. The truth was that I was nutty as a fruitcake at the same time.

Religion is a common theme for the mentally ill, and persons with bipolar disorder are no different. The disorder allowed me to have great confidence in the truth of the Bible and insight into that truth. I ran a good Bible study and found the scriptures live and vibrant. I was certain that my loathsome symptoms, particularly anxiety and my depressed mood, were going to be healed. I would not have described myself as an emotional believer. I felt firm and grounded in the faith.

Lithium smashed all of that like an aluminum can crusher. As rapidly as it changed my mind and my symptoms, it robbed me of my enthusiastic faith. Within weeks I watched in horror as I became less and less the man of God I felt I had been. I didn't know where it would stop, and I didn't dare tell anyone, especially your mom. I have years of prayer lists and Bible study notes that refer to every spiritual topic, including my fears and anxiety, and they all come to a grinding halt the month after my diagnosis and starting lithium.

This is difficult to describe. I don't know anyone who has ever been through this experience. I know my faith wasn't based on my manic emotions. Yet without my emotional tie it suddenly seemed flat and lifeless. The scriptures became hard to read, and Jesus no longer seemed like my closest friend. God felt distant. Did everything just go away? No. My intellectual grasp of Christianity did not falter. Truth remained true, and I never quit believing. I was just different.

I quit teaching my Bible study at church. I quit feeling like attending church. I felt removed from the whole body of believers. I thought about artists and writers and composers and all the famous people I was learning about who suffered from bipolar disorder. The modern ones all wrote of a fear of drug therapy. They feared the loss of drive and passion and creativity. That is a genuine fear based in reality. I could not take lithium and be the same person. Much of the bad stuff was going away, but along with it seemed to go some of the good stuff, the passion and emotional energy I had lived with in my Christianity.

That was almost twenty years ago. I've never regained that passion or emotional ground. I've become a much more settled and, for lack of a better word, intellectual believer. I'm no less conservative and much more convinced of the truth of the Bible and salvation through Jesus. But I don't feel it. I never have again. I prefer quiet churches without clapping and hand raising, and I prefer old liturgy. Frankly, I don't like attending church at all. Was all of that fervor at the time false or fake? I don't think so. Bipolar mania exaggerated my personal traits, both good and bad. I was emotional about spiritual things, and what emotions I had were developed more highly with the mania. My mania sharpened my emotional edge. I've taught Bible studies again and have been good at it. At one time I became active in a church and contributed much to it.

Faith is a funny thing. It involves the spirit and the soul of a person. In my case my soul or body is a flawed one and susceptible to mental illness. My loss of an emotional tie to my faith was collateral damage from medications. It remains a casualty.

Your loving father,
Dad

Mental Illness And Faith

Dear Matt,

I imagine you have reflected at some time on the relationship of Christianity and mental illness. I think about it often. It is a religion that places a lot of emphasis on personal responsibility coupled with God's grace: his unmerited favor toward persons. Both are important issues when you are mentally ill.

It is very easy to get caught up in the idea that your mind is nothing more than a bunch of chemical connections to nerves and what little is left is your upbringing and learned behaviors. I'm convinced that the mind cannot be explained away in simple chemical terms. There is room for choices and creativity and a thousand other things that are not just emotional but spiritual. We were made in the image of God, and I know God's mind is more than a batch of nerve transmitters running about. Still, the power of the mind is easy to underestimate. Mentally ill people don't underestimate it; we know how powerful it is and how much of it is chemically driven. But I am glad to know that I am more than just a bag of chemicals and nerve transmitters.

I have had periods of time in my life when I could not be held responsible for my actions or thoughts. Even now small parts of me don't work right, and I cannot change them. A lot of my mind, maybe most of my mind, works well now. I'm not entirely under the control of my disorder anymore. I have genuine faith. But how will God deal with me in my mentally flawed and at times out-of-control state?

Bible models have been helpful to me. One of my favorite passages in the Bible concerns the crazy man in the land of the Gerasenes. He lived in the tombs and had Herculean strength. Friends and family had abandoned him. He was a homeless mentally ill person. Jesus's response to this man when he came howling up to Jesus was to heal him of his illness. The next verses show him seated at the feet of Jesus in his right mind and "fully clothed." That is how I want to be as a mentally ill believer: fully clothed. To me that signifies completeness and dignity. Jesus restored this guy fully to normality and even saw to it that he had clothes. No more shame of nakedness.

In what ways am I like the crazy man who can't be held responsible for his actions and thoughts, and in what ways am I just a normal man with a sinful nature who acts sinfully? Is there a dividing line that can be discerned? I've never been able to discern it, and I think that is the crux of the matter. It is important because I am probably both the crazy and the sane man at the same time. I will be held responsible for some of what I am and what I do, but part of me has to be accepted as I am: mentally flawed. Does that make sense? I just don't know what parts are which. Perhaps it doesn't matter whether I know. That is where my hope in grace comes in.

Will God's favor toward me be sufficient for my crazy side? I think so. Jesus didn't get into it with the crazy Gerasene man any more than he did with any of the crazy persons he encountered. He freely healed them. More often than not he restored normality for the persons he healed. As a friend has said, Jesus used miracles to restore persons to their routine and ordinary lives. Routine and ordinary sounds good to me.

Your loving father,
Dad

Normal Days In The Whirligig

Dear Matt,

I have normal days now. I'll go further than that. I mostly have days that follow one another without much change from one day to the next. That is a big deal to me. That means I'm finally stable. There is predictability to my life. Predictably I'll be the same person tomorrow that I am today. Predictability is something bipolar persons don't take for granted. You cannot imagine how important it is to your mom that she can count on me being pretty much the same guy day to day.

I have symptoms of bipolar disorder every day. I am always depressed to some degree. I'm rarely entirely free of anxiety. I can slip into one crazy scheme or another easily. Paradoxically, I think the side effects of my medications are almost as bad as the disease now. I feel flat and lazy. Fatigue is a real problem. I feel a loss of creativity and a nagging inertia. I get diarrhea. One of the most troublesome side effects is akathisia, a feeling of internal restlessness and need to move around. It makes sitting through a movie difficult.

My symptoms have cycles. We can almost tell the season by the cycle. I have more depression than anything through the winter months and the holidays. Late in the spring and into the summer I can be counted on to accelerate. I've always spent money or bought new cars late in the summer. My medications get kicked up, and your mom becomes more vigilant in watching for crazy behavior and moods. Then come the fall glooms, when I become restless and irritable. Predictably, winter rolls around, and my anxiety drops further down to normal for me. I get a break on my medication doses. I still don't like Christmas.

Within these cycles I retain my predictability. It may be that I'm different in October than May, but I'm consistent in mood and mind within those months. If I didn't know better I wouldn't call this stability, but in comparison to the many dark years I've lived through I'm rock solid. But this is a disorder marked by its cycles, and even though I have a mixed form I am still prone to cycling. The burden of my days has been mostly lifted.

I've not become a bore, but I do try to maintain routine. I can always be found at the same coffee shops and cafes like DG's Deli at the same times on the same days, week after week. Your mom and I eat out every Saturday morning at Durango Bagels. I always eat the same meal. I enjoy coffee at Milagro Coffee y Espresso Saturday afternoons and a different one Sunday morning. Your mom and I always have coffee together Sunday afternoon. I go from work to home and home to work. I don't do much else anymore. No more ambulance chasing or lawyer sparring. I have only two jobs. I still teach part-time in the community college in addition to my clinic duties.

Compared to my wild days I have settled down almost too much. Not every day in the past was bad or every week regrettable. On the whole I still made quite a mess of things, but life is much tamer now.

Your loving father,
Dad

Not The End

Dear Matt,

So there it is. From start to a near finish I think I've summed up the decades of mental illness I've experienced and shared with you. Up until recently, life has been a job of hanging onto the monkey bars. I could move any direction I wanted: up, down, left, or right. I could go in directions very few could follow. The problem has always been one of not falling. I've had drops from time to time. I've picked up this book over the years but could never keep mentally together long enough to make much progress. I thought about just sending the letters to you as I went along, hoping that would produce a manuscript. The last couple of years of stability have given me a chance to finally make these letters one piece of work. There have been breaks while my moods took vacations

I've found that adequately communicating to you about the times of madness was difficult. I was rarely in a mind-set that allowed for good future recollection. I think I've got things right this time. I've stuck to the stories I remember well. There are events that are too vague to recall or too embarrassing to write about. You are a smart kid. I don't doubt for a minute that you have your own recollections and can fill in many blanks. Hopefully I've filled in many of the blanks for you. I've had some terrible ups and downs, but one thing I've learned while writing to you is how much I've improved over the years and how much more mundane my illness has become. We've come close to closing the chasm in my mind.

I don't know how many persons with bipolar disorder have been blessed by the kind of persons who have surrounded me during my adult years. You kids have been no small part of that cadre. Raising children, however limited my role was for years, has been one of the great parts of my life. You have all shown the capacity to accept me largely the way I was and the way I am. Your mother deserves sainthood. It appears to me that at every critical turn in the road during my worst of times someone has popped up to help me through the rapids. I hope everyone I've mentioned can sense my gratitude.

All of you will have to deal at some time with your dysfunctional upbringing and my substantial contribution to that. There are going to be therapy bills. It has always been a joke among us that we would help pay for the first year of each of your turns in therapy. It is only half a joke. Part of this relates to the intense self-focus of a mental illness. I was so locked into my own mind and problems for so many years. I'm finally better about that now, a bit late in the game for you.

I imagine child rearing will bring out the toughest of struggles with your upbringing. There is nothing quite like it to make you look back and wonder why you do things the way you do. We've helped form many of your preferences, some of which you would probably like to do without.

I'll always be your father, crazy or not. We've had some wonderful times together, and living with a manic dad is not always such a bad deal. You've enjoyed a host of experiences and objects that you would never have enjoyed had I been an ordinary father. Disaster was never far from us, but it never materialized. We've always been able to pull up while I've been diving for the tarmac.

I love each of you dearly. I love and admire your mother beyond words. I hope we can enjoy these better years together. I think we will, partially because of the many odd years we did have together. I'm sorry again for the lousy financial support you've had. Perhaps I should not be so regretful of the emotional and mental inheritance you have from me. In some ways you may have had better training for life than you would have had otherwise. It is a crazy world out there, and you know craziness well.

I have all of you to thank for seeing me to this point in my life. I have friends who have stood by me and helped me when I needed it. Near strangers and hired professionals deserve my thanks. Your mother deserves many years of a sane and predictable life. I'm grateful to God. Now that I have this little window of clear retrospective, I'm not sure that I would have wanted to have a different life than I've been given. Like a lifelong inmate who is contemplating prison release, I wouldn't know how to live. This is the only life I've known.

Your loving father,
Dad